MW00830075

Anointed to Do Good

Acts 10:38
Insights into Building, Maintaining,
and Releasing God's Anointing
in Your Life and Ministry

Dr. Keith Attles

ISBN 978-1-63903-153-5 (paperback)
ISBN 978-1-63903-154-2 (digital)

Copyright © 2021 by Dr. Keith Attles

All rights reserved. No part of this publication may be reproduced, distributed, or transmitted in any form or by any means, including photocopying, recording, or other electronic or mechanical methods without the prior written permission of the publisher. For permission requests, solicit the publisher via the address below.

Christian Faith Publishing, Inc.
832 Park Avenue
Meadville, PA 16335
www.christianfaithpublishing.com

Printed in the United States of America

Contents

———— ❦ ————

Acknowledgments

⸻

I am grateful for the foundation given to me by my father, Thomas Attles, and my mother, Jean Attles, as they always sought to make me a man of God. My sisters, Michelle and Lisa, have proven to be a source of support and inspiration for me as I continue to grow in the grace and anointing of the Lord.

I sincerely thank God for the entire Covenant Life Ministries Church family's dedication and prayerful support, which constantly empowered me through the difficult times along the way. I wish God's blessing on each of you.

Finally, and most importantly, a heartfelt thank you to my wife, Kimberly, and three children, Aaron, Daniel, and Alisa, who helped me to write this book because of their sacrificial love, patience, and prayers. They gave me the time to complete this research by handling many of my home and church responsibilities through the duration of the writing process. I love and appreciate you all. May God richly bless you.

Preface

━━━━━━━ ❦ ━━━━━━━

*A*nointed to Do Good is a resource designed to educate, enhance, and ultimately empower a believer to do anointed ministry by the power of the Holy Spirit. It is my personal conviction that many believers and churches have sought to do ministry apart from the Holy Spirit's enablement primarily because we have been convinced that education, programming, or traditional systems promoting church life are enough to "get the job done" for God's kingdom. Jesus Christ, the Son of God, left for us an example to follow in Matthew 3:15–17, which patterned for us the need for God's Holy Spirit (the anointing), in order to produce greater results in life and ministry.

The anointing of the Holy Spirit will be examined through various lenses, giving the reader a rich understanding of a misunderstood topic in the Body of Christ. My goal is to create a fresh hunger in the life of every believer who desires to grow in the depths of God's anointing and to produce fruitful results for the expansion of God's kingdom. An especially insightful section of this workbook is the *Devotionals*. The *Devotionals* are designed to encourage the believer in weekly spiritual practices. I recommend that you choose one or two devotionals that you plan to practice during the week and follow the reading, reflection questions, and spiritual practices carefully. If these directives are followed, you will begin to experience a deeper spiritual life in the Lord; as well as a walk in a greater anointing of the Holy Spirit.

You can change the world for Christ under the anointing of the Holy Spirit. May God richly bless you.

Rev. Dr. Keith Attles

Christian Spirituality
A Historical Overview

F or many years, I have often wondered why the church of today did not really model the Apostolic Church found in the book of Acts. This question provoked me to search for answers in church history writings throughout many generations. What I have found was the church Christ came to establish and sought to fulfill a different mandate than the one we see today. The early church stressed the "Great Commission" (Matthew 28:18–20) as its main reason for existence, coupled with the empowerment of the Holy Spirit with signs, wonders, and miracles following. The purpose of the church was to exhibit power over all the kingdoms of Satan by setting the captives free so that they could be able to serve the living God.

As the Apostolic Church moved into different parts of the world, its doctrine became tainted and weakened because of pagan philosophy and practices, which de-emphasized the teachings of the kingdom of God and the person of the Holy Spirit. By AD 313, Constantine became ruler of the Roman Empire and chose Christianity as the state religion. Little by little, the state began to take control of the affairs of the Apostolic Church, and leaders with little or no experience in religious matters began to shape Church doctrine. About AD 350, the Church began to persecute all who were not under the authority of the Roman Catholic Church. People had to make the choice of submitting to the Church or face the sword. Salvation with the need for "justification by faith," culminating in the "new birth" experience, was no longer emphasized. Hence, the imperial church of Constantine continued to become increasingly distant from the original purpose Christ intended when He established His church. This led to the Medieval Church period (AD 476–1453), which lasted for about one thousand years. This period is better known as the "Dark Ages" of history because gross darkness began to influence both political and religious leadership during this time. Corruption within the Roman Catholic Church became very apparent with the selling of indulgences, the extortion of finances from both the rich and poor to finance the church, and the distortion of sound Christian doctrine with teachings on transubstantiation (in the communion sacrament, the bread and wine are transformed into the veritable body and blood of Christ). These types of corrupt practices in the church caused men like John Wycliffe (1329–1384), John Huss (1369–1415), and Jerome Savonarola (1452–1498) to arise and proclaim the injustices advocated by Roman Catholicism.

Later, after the fall of Constantinople in 1453, the Church was positioned to receive revival and enlightenment from men whom the Holy Spirit would move upon in order to right the wrongs that cast it into the "Dark Ages." Over a two-hundred-year period, a great reformation began to take place, which started in Germany and spread all throughout Northern Europe. This resulted in the founding of national churches owing no allegiance to Rome. Much of the transitional period of the church called the "Reformation" was attributed to a man named Martin Luther, who was a monk and professor at the University of Wittenberg. Luther observed many of the practices advocated by Roman Catholicism and concluded that these theological beliefs and practices were not in-line with the Word of God. Men could not be justified by works of obedience as preached by John Tetzel who sold certificates to pardon all sin. Martin Luther vehemently protested against such doctrine and set out to disprove this type of flawed teaching. On October 31, 1517, Luther nailed his "Ninety-five Theses" or statements to the front door of the Wittenberg Cathedral, openly protesting the selling of indulgences and his discontentment with the Pope and priesthood. He maintained that many doctrines and practices of the church were not consistent with the Holy Scriptures. Although certain rulers within the church tried to coerce Luther into recanting these statements, he held firm to his convictions and beliefs. The writings of Luther spread throughout Germany, and many people who were discontent with the Catholic Church soon found themselves siding with his views in "protest" against this erroneous religious system. Hence, the title "Protestants" were given to his followers and a major division occurred in the Christian faith. No longer would there be only the Catholic Church, but now there would also be the Protestant Church alongside it. The church that had existed for hundreds of years in darkness was now about to be given a ray of light through the efforts of an enlightened man named Martin Luther, the father of the Protestant Reformation period.

The works and writings of Luther did not go unnoticed in the church community. Soon the reformation in Germany spread all over Europe. In Switzerland, Ulrich Zwingli, in 1517, protested against the "remission of sins" through pilgrimages to a shrine of the Virgin at Einsiedeln and, in 1522, broke from Roman Catholicism. John Calvin, William Tyndale, John Knox, the Quakers, and John Wesley were among the major contributors of the Protestant Reformation, which later influenced other countries all over the world.

During the early years of the Protestant Reformation, three major concerns needed to be addressed. The first was the right of the followers of Jesus Christ to have the ability to read and study the Scriptures for themselves in a "known" language. Second was to rid the church of corrupt leadership, doctrine, and practices. Third was an emphasis on holy living and seeking communion with the Holy Spirit in order to empower the believer for everyday living. Personal edification and growth was what this movement was all about.

The Medieval Church had awesome structure, liturgy, and beauty attributed to its movement, but the Protestant Church produced power in the lives of its followers. As the church of Jesus Christ continued to experience change and transformation back to his intended purposes for its existence, a new era arose for the church called the "Modern Church" era. This era, which began about AD 1453 to the present, seemed to be used by God to get the church back to how it began in AD 30 as the Apostolic Church. Jesus Christ has allowed the Holy Spirit to bring fresh revelation and insight to men that were responsive to bring about seasons of restoration and revival to the church. Men like Martin Luther and John Wesley were able to capture the leading of God's Spirit, concerning what needed to be emphasized for the preservation of the church throughout history.

I believe that success of the church during the present modern era will hinge on the efforts of the Holy Spirit trying to convey to the hearts of men to follow His leading. The Holy Spirit must be allowed to communicate to church leaders the mind of God for the purpose of seeing it return to the glory of the Apostolic Church, a church of power and purpose. Many of our church fathers were not afraid of allowing the Holy Spirit to dictate what needed to be addressed as the church continued to move in progressive revelation. This type of revelation comes by following very closely the leading of the Holy Spirit as He reveals present-day truth to impact our generation. The Spirit of God is endeavoring to produce a glorious church and people if we would only listen and obey as many have done in the past. We are desperately in need of revival and renewal in the church and America; no longer can believers afford to walk in darkness as the church did centuries ago.

The first Great Awakening occurred around the early 1700s under the leadership of Johnathan Edwards (1703–1758), which caused an awesome revival that spread throughout all the American colonies. A Second Great Awakening began in the Cane Ridge, Kentucky, area in 1801. Many believers experienced a renewed interest in Christian devotion and living that was brought about by an emphasis on repentance from sinful practices. As a result, there was an unusual outpouring of the Holy Spirit with accompanying signs and wonders. Many who were touched by the Holy Spirit exhibited manifestations like jerking, rolling, and dancing during revival meetings.

Once again, around 1906, God poured out His Spirit as evidenced in the Azusa Street Mission of Los Angeles. The Pentecostal Fire of this movement spread all over America, which broke down many of the racial and denominational barriers that existed during this time. Believers from all walks of life received the baptism in the

Holy Spirit with the evidence of speaking in tongues. The Church in America was beginning to transition out of the Modern Church era back to its origin of beginnings, hence, the Apostolic Church. Signs once again were becoming commonplace in the existence of the church.

As we begin a new decade (AD 2000), our expectation should be to position ourselves for another great move of the Holy Spirit in our generation. In the 1700s, 1800s, and 1900s, God had chosen to awaken His church with a mighty demonstration of His spirit. Position yourself and get ready for a fresh anointing by the Holy Spirit.

Jesus spoke, concerning the "last days" upon the earth, just before His coming. He said in Matthew 24 and 25, that it would be characterized by lawlessness, ungodliness, unbelief, and a host of other sins. The Apostle Paul wrote in 2 Timothy 3:1–9 how the last days would encompass everything Jesus spoke about and a lot more as detailed in His letter to Timothy. Both servants of God were able to foresee the drastic changes in men's hearts, which would ultimately cause tremendous social breakdowns in relationships at every level in society. These predictions serve to notify believers of the pending decline in moral and ethical conduct, thus, resulting in judgment upon all sin.

Kingdoms in Conflict

Since the beginning of time, with the creation of man, there has always been an unseen battle being waged between forces of good and evil. Both of these forces have identified rulers over their respective kingdoms through which they exercise their dominion and power. In the process of time, Scripture tells us how God (the ruler of good) planted a garden in a place called Eden. His purpose was to create a beautiful place of habitation for His created beings, Adam and Eve (Genesis 2:1–15). God had made Adam and Eve to be in His image and after this likeness (Genesis 1:26), and to literally be an extension of His power and authority on the earth (Genesis 1:26–28) by giving them dominion. God's great love over His crowning piece of creation (Psalm 8:4–6) provoked Satan (the ruler of evil) to arise with strong opposition against the plan of God. This led Satan to go on the offensive attack by using trickery, lies, and deception as his weaponry in order to destroy mankind (Genesis 3:1–7).

Before this attack ever took place, God gave very specific commands to Adam regarding the "tree in the midst of the garden, the tree of the knowledge of good and evil." Adam understood the boundaries God established for his peace, security, and longevity while dwelling in Eden, but Satan (the tempter) cunningly manipulated the words of God and deceived Eve. Adam should have taken dominion over Satan with the delegated authority God had originally invested in him (Genesis 1:26–28), but instead he remained very quiet as Eve is deceived (Genesis 3:6). Adam's disobedience to the Lord is how the spiritual dispute between God and Satan spilled over into the natural realm here on earth. Adam's disobedience opened the door to sin, which has ultimately left man separated from God—sick, alone, powerless, and defeated in this life.

Our God, who is rich in mercy, would not allow His enemy to remain victorious over His creation for long. As soon as Adam and Eve fell, God immediately spoke a prophetic word concerning a coming deliverer who would, once and for all, crush the authority of the opposing kingdom in Genesis 3:15. This coming deliverer would break the bondage of sin over mankind and allow them once again to experience intimate fellowship with their God. Jesus the Messiah (the Anointed One) was to be born of a virgin birth in a little town called Bethlehem located in Jerusalem. This "Genesis 3:15" deliverer was born to do only one thing—that was to destroy the works of the enemy, Satan (1 John 3:8).

The Ministry of Jesus

For about thirty years, Scripture tells us that Jesus, during this time, grew in favor with both God and man (Luke 1:80, Luke 2:40, 52) until the day of His showing. There are no records of Him doing anything significant like casting out devils or performing any miracles until the ministry of John the Baptist was fulfilled. In Matthew

3:13–17, John's ministry is nearing its conclusion, and we see the Holy Spirit confirming Jesus as both the Savior and Deliverer of humanity. Following Christ's baptism and inauguration into ministry, He is immediately challenged by Satan to relinquish His position of power and authority and disobey the purposes of God. By using temptation and deception with Adam and Eve, Satan now tries to duplicate these same tactics with Jesus to no avail (Matthew 4:1–11). Christ withstands every attempt to cause Him to sin against his Father. Two opposing kingdoms clashed, and the kingdom of God prevailed. Jesus was now qualified to become the Savior/Deliverer of the world. After many seasons of preparation and temptation, Jesus begins His ministry under the power of the Holy Spirit. His three main objectives are to destroy the works of the devil, to provide salvation to all who are lost, and to establish His kingdom on earth. Jesus accomplished this by (Matthew 4:23–25, Mark 1:38–39, Luke 4:43)

1. preaching the Gospel (Good News) of the kingdom (the rule, reign, and authority) of God,
2. telling people to repent and believe the Gospel,
3. going into cities and towns (where there were masses of hurting people),
4. demonstrating the power and authority of the kingdom by casting out devils, and
5. performing miracles and healing amongst the sick and oppressed (Acts 10:38),

Every time Jesus preached, healed, or cast out a devil, He was literally proclaiming that the King's kingdom and authority were now present in *bodily form* (Colossians 2:8) to overthrow the powers of darkness. This type of militant attitude was evident throughout Jesus's ministry because He fully understood the magnitude of spiritual warfare in which He was engaged. For this reason, Jesus chose disciples in whom He was going to invest His entire life. He asked them to give up everything and to follow Him unconditionally no matter what the cost (Matthew 4:18–20, Luke 9:62). Anyone who was to be involved with establishing kingdom power and authority in the earth had to be willing to deny himself of worldly pleasures (Matthew 16:24) in order to totally follow Christ. These are the types of individuals Jesus needed to be able to establish His Church before He went to the cross.

The Purpose of the Church

Jesus's life and ministry always revealed the two most important reasons why He was born in the earth. The first was to give His life as a "ransom for many" (Matthew 20:28) so that through Him, the world might be saved (John 3:16–17) by way of the cross (Ephesians 2:14–16, 1 Corinthians 1:18, Philippians 2:8). Second, Christ came to establish His church. In Matthew 16, we read how Peter received the revelation of who Jesus was when He said, "Thou art the Christ, the Son of the living God." In response to Peter's revelation, Jesus tells His disciples that Peter would be the rock upon which He would establish His church, and that hell itself would not be able to stop its advancement (Matthew 16:15–18). Christ's goal was to create an institution on earth that would further advance His Father's kingdom once He completed His work on earth. The Church was and is that vehicle established to replicate the life and ministry of Jesus Christ.

Jesus not only wanted His church to preach His message, "Repent for the kingdom of God is at hand" (Mark 1:15) but also to demonstrate His power and authority over the Satanic kingdom. For this cause, Christ said in Matthew 16:19 that He would give His Church the "keys to the kingdom of heaven" and the authority to open and close (to declare forbidden or to declare allowed) both heaven and earth by the power of the Holy Spirit. The same ability Jesus possessed was now being transferred to His Church. Until now the followers of Jesus were being trained to duplicate His ministry of healing the sick, casting out devils, preaching to the poor, raising the dead, and opening blinded eyes (Mark 6:6–13), Luke 10:1–20, and Luke 7:19–22).

All that Jesus envisioned was now ready to become a reality. In Acts 2, the Holy Spirit (the empowerment of God) was given to His followers (the Church) for the purpose of delivering humanity from the bondage of satanic rule and control. The Church has been called by God to continue to destroy the works of the devil and to advance the kingdom of God (Mark 16:15–18), thus becoming an instrument of "deliverance" to captive individuals.

The confrontation between good and evil, love and hate, the church and this world system are speedily reaching their conclusion. As we readily see these prophetic predictions coming to pass, the church must finally decide whose side it is on. This is not a current situation believers find themselves in, but in fact, this has always been a challenge for all who have followed the Lord. Adam, Noah, Abraham, David, and the nation of Israel had to always decide which side they belonged. In Exodus 32:11–35, we have an account of Moses returning from the top of Mount Sinai with the Ten Commandments and finding the children of Israel engaging in immoral behavior. This caused Moses to ask the question, "Who is on the Lord's side?" (vs. 26), which helped to determine those individuals fully committed to the Lord and His servant. The tribe of Levi responded to the question by siding with Moses and slaying about three thousand men because of their sin (vs. 28).

Another powerful story in the Old Testament that communicates the reality of God's people making a conscious decision to side with the Lord is found in 1 Kings 18:15–40. Here, Elijah the prophet challenged the four hundred and fifty prophets of Baal and four hundred prophets of the "groves" (Hebrew Asherah, a Canaanite goddess) to an open contest on Mount Carmel. This was done to determine who the more powerful god was and whom the people should follow. The eight hundred and fifty false prophets were defeated by one true prophet of God, and hundreds of people were convinced to side with the Lord. The miraculous demonstration of power by Elijah ultimately changed the hearts of the people as they watched fire fall from heaven to consume the sacrifice and altar (vs. 31–39). Both of these events clearly illustrate the need and command for God's people to willingly choose to serve Him with all their heart. This means that if we are to escape the contamination of this present age, one must daily choose to "present your body as a living sacrifice, holy, acceptable unto God" (Romans 12:1). My entire life needs to be submitted to the will of God instead of the dictates of the world. These choices are not at all easy for any of us to make, but with the grace of God working in our hearts, we can prevail. Second Peter 1:10 assures us if we allow our walk in the Lord to consistently progress, we have no need of being overly concerned with stumbling or failing in our Christian service to God. This assurance can be acquired by obtaining a fuller knowledge of God and Jesus our Lord through studying and allowing His grace and peace to be revealed in our hearts. The revelation of His divine nature (vs. 4) present in us is obtained by knowing, understanding, and acting upon His "exceeding great and precious promises," which have been given throughout the scriptures.

When a child of God chooses to yield their mind, body, and spirit to the Lord, they then become empowered to withstand seducing (misleading) spirits and doctrines (teachings) of devils (demons) (1 Timothy 4:1) that have increased in activity in these last days (1 Timothy 3:1). We need to be able to say like Joshua, "As for me and my house, we will serve the Lord" (Joshua 24:15). This pledge of allegiance to the Lord is the kind of commitment we must make if we are to overcome the powers of darkness in this evil day.

Biblical and Historical Character/ Spiritual Formation Models

— ✑ —

C haracter development, spiritual formation, and Christlikeness are interchangeable terms, which focus on transforming the "inner man" of a follower of Christ into the image of God. Throughout biblical and church history, both leaders and Christians alike sought methods, disciplines, and practices to better reflect God's nature and essence in their daily lives. This pursuit has created many traditions, denominations, and even cults over an extended period of time, including both testaments.

In the New Testament, spiritual formation was of great importance to the apostles and early church fathers due to their commitment of transforming believers into Christ's image and for making disciples. Craig A. Blasing, a professor of systematic theology at the Southern Baptist Theological Seminary, noted how the early Christians were constantly involved in meeting regularly for prayer, instruction in the Scriptures, living in the Spirit, growing in faith and love, and maintaining a hope in the coming of the Lord.[1] These practices were believed to provide a firm foundation in the Christian faith, but within less than one hundred years since the birth of Christianity, new followers of Jesus Christ found themselves embracing doctrines other than those of Christ. As the church started to spread throughout "the world," social status and geographical loca-

---

[1] Kenneth O. Gangel and James C. Wilhoit, *The Christian Educator's Handbook on Spiritual Formation*, (Grand Rapids: Baker Books, 1994), 21.

tion played a major role in how much of Christ's and the apostles' teachings were being followed.

Blasing comments by saying, "Some form of pagan religion, whether a local cult, a particular mystery religion, imperial religious rites, popular Hellenistic polytheism, magic, astrology, or most likely some combination of these," ultimately influenced the purity of the teachings of Christ. Gnostic cults flourished in the second century with a distorted or syncretized message, which hindered a believer's growth and development in the faith. For this reason, Blasing says,

> A Christian minister in the late second century needed to closely question a pagan who wanted to become a Christian, professed to believe in God or in Christ, or wanted to be baptized, because for many a professed faith in Christ was just an element added to their syncretistic faith. Conversion involved a total transformation of worldview, of self-understanding, and a complete new set of social relationships.[2]

For these reasons, the Church created new forms for ministry, worship, and instruction in the teachings of Christ in order to produce a purer faith and godly life within believers. The second century of Christianity unveiled an intentional model for spiritual formation, which also targeted the character and life of Christ imparted into believers as a whole. "Spiritual formation began with enrollment into the catechumenate the ranks of those preparing for baptism." Blasing continues, "The catechumens were instructed in Christian character and all aspects of their lives examined with respect to the faith."[3] The process of spiritual/character formation continued for hundreds of years over the course of church history. This gave rise to many for-

---

[2] Kenneth O. Gangel and James C. Wilhoit, *The Christian Educator's Handbook on Spiritual Formation*, (Grand Rapids: Baker Books, 1994), 22.

[3] Kenneth O. Gangel and James C. Wilhoit, *The Christian Educator's Handbook on Spiritual Formation*, (Grand Rapids: Baker Books, 1994), 23–24.

mats, methods, and practices, some being sound doctrinally, while others proved cultic and heretical over the duration of time.

After the deaths of the original apostles, the early church fathers sought to maintain the sound tenets of the faith by implementing strict observances to the teachings of the Church. As the gospel spread, pagan religions and practices threatened the quality of Christian values, thus, causing a severe reaction by the Church's leadership to resolve the problem. This gave rise to aesthetic practices within the Church in order to preserve character/spiritual formation amongst its current and new believers.

Author Keith Beasley-Topliffe in his book defines asceticism by saying, "The term asceticism comes from the Greek root '*askesis*' referring to discipline, training, or exercises."

The New Testament uses two other Greek words in a similar way. One *paideia* (from paides, "children") refers to pedagogical methods akin to what Plato meant by "the education of desire" (Hebrew 12:8, 11, 2 Timothy 3:16).

> A second key word for discipline is related to the word *gymnasium*. Like a Greek athlete who would exercise naked (gymnazo), "training in godliness" requires a kind of spiritual stripping down (1 Timothy 4:7–8, Hebrew 12:11).[4]

The main goal of this kind of practice was to encourage austere self-discipline, which was voluntarily in order to achieve a higher spiritual ideal. Hence, within the early church, this Greek mindset crept into the doctrines of Scripture (note Paul's references in 1 Corinthians 9:24–27, Galatians 2:2, Philippians 2:16), and within the writings of the church fathers such as the shepherd of Hermas, Barnabas, Tatian, and Ignatius of Antioch.[5] As a concern for moral

---

[4] Keith Beasley-Topliffe, *The Upper Room Dictionary of Christian Spiritual Formation*. Nashville: Upper Room Books, 2003.

[5] Urban T. Holmes III, *History of Christian Spirituality: An Analytical Introduction*. Harrisburg: Morehouse Publishing, 2002, 22–23.

purity grew, the Church found itself drifting into greater levels of self-denial practices, which led to martyrdom, Encratism, and even monasticism. The Greek meaning of "encratic" is "self-controlled or disciplined." If you were a follower of this belief system, extreme practices would often be displayed to show your level of commitment to the Lord. "One of the practices of the Encratites was self-castration, celebrated corporately on occasion by running through the streets holding one's testicles aloft."[6] This type of renunciation of the physical body and worldly pleasures eventually gave way to a monastic lifestyle as believers sought to sanctify themselves from a polluted society.

> By the time the Roman emperor Constantine endorsed Christianity in 314, many Christians were acquiring wealth. Yet other individuals and small groups desired a simple life and so fled to wilderness areas of Egypt in the third and fourth centuries. Desert silence provided a spiritual gymnasium for the desert fathers and mothers to become true athletes of God. Benedict of Nursia wrote his Rule to establish healthy monastic communities. Francis of Assisi combined personal stripping of wealth with social concern for the poor.[7]

This quote from Beasley-Topliffe's book provides some insight into the minds of early Christians and their intent to remain set apart for the purposes of God. The answer to growing in faith and holiness for believers during this period of time was to practice *anchoritism*, which in Greek means "to withdraw." For the sake of escaping martyrdom and to respond to God's call to "be perfect" (Matthew 5:48), many believers gave themselves over to prayer and service,

---

6 Ibid, 22–23.
7 Keith Beasley-Topliffe, *The Upper Room Dictionary of Christian Spiritual Formation*. Nashville: Upper Room Books, 2003, 25.

whether alone or in community. Leaders such as Evagrius Ponticus, John Climacus (John of the Ladder), Gregory of Nazianzen, even Gregory of Nyssa, and many others arose to the challenge of guarding the sanctity of Christian life. One of the greatest contributors to this movement and regarded as one of the most influential Church leaders ever was Saint Augustine (354–430), the bishop of Hippo and doctor of the Latin church. Saint Augustine formed a religious community in North Africa where he lived for thirty-four years in a monastic community. It was there that he struggled with the "inner self" as he sought to understand the mind, will, and body and its effect on a believer's relationship to God and Christ. His thoughts and reflection on this topic were written in his autobiographical work entitled, *Confessions*.[8] As the church continued to move forward throughout history, the Middle Ages produced people like Gregory the Great, Maximus the Confessor, Bernard of Clairvaux, Francis of Assisi, and Thomas Aquinas, who sought to enhance the believer's walk with God by either adding to or subtracting from the practice of asceticism. The Late Middle Ages (1300–1500) to the fifteenth century paved the way for monasticism's growth, along with a group of people known as mystics during this period. The search to understand God's mystery and plan for life caused many to get involved in mysticism, which is "a spirituality grounded in radical openness to the divine mystery."[9] Christian mysticism seeks to create a union with God by being open to various ways of communication (affective, sexual, familial, and artistic) as the Holy Spirit assists in this endeavor.[10]

As the Christian character/spiritual formation movement progressed, it gave way to the modern period that introduced people like Ignatius Loyola, Teresa of Avila, and John of the Cross, who were of the Spanish school of thought regarding spirituality. These

---

[8] Richard J. Foster, and James B. Smith. *Devotional Classics: Selected Readings for Individuals and Groups.* San Francisco: Harper Collins, 2005, 55.

[9] Keith Beasley-Topliffe, *The Upper Room Dictionary of Christian Spiritual Formation. Nashville:* Upper Room Books, 2003, 195.

[10] Ibid, 195.

individuals during the "Age of Reason" sought to introduce the "first science of the spiritual life." According to Dr. Urban Holmes, he says, "Scientific spirituality means a systematic analysis of the totality of the spiritual experience with the intention of describing both the means and ends of that experience in such a way that it can be taught and followed, as well as compared with other systems."[11]

The ability to create a methodology for character/spiritual formation paved the way for some emerging church leaders to provide educational-systematic forums in developing a transformational Christian lifestyle. In addition to the Spanish school, there were contributions made by Italian, French, and English schools, which produced various systems and methodologies over the next few hundred years in church history. As the emphasis continued to develop concerning character/spiritual formation during the sixteenth century, it allowed for the birth of Protestantism led by Martin Luther. He reintroduced a belief in the "priesthood of all believers" as a foundational doctrine of the church. His teaching concerning this topic "opened up a theological basis for a genuine lay spirituality unknown since patristic times."[12] No longer was the necessity for spiritual development relegated to the clergy alone, but any follower of Christ was encouraged to grow spiritually in Christ for the purpose of serving him. Next, we have the teachings of John Calvin as a major influence during the beginning stages Protestantism. Calvin was a rationalist who rejected pilgrimages, fasting, almsgiving, and other ascetical practices. Therefore, he believed that piety was a characteristic of the person who lived within the order of God. "Piety is grounded in a sense of dependence and reveals itself in service and worship. The pious person is obedient to God's law and loves his fellows. He is dutiful in meditation and prayer."[13] John Calvin saw spirituality more of an intellectual than effectual experience in a believer's life in Christ. Perhaps one of the most influential Christian leaders to

---

[11] Urban T. Holmes III, *A History of Christian Spirituality: An Analytical Introduction.* Harrisburg: Morehouse Publishing, 2002, 93.

[12] Ibid, 126.

[13] Ibid, 127.

emerge over the next few decades was Philipp Jakob Spener (1635–1705) who was considered by many to be the "father of Pietism." Spener was a German pastor who wrote, *Pia Desideria*, which was aimed at improving the Protestant Church's heartfelt desire for piety by pressing the need for repentance and rebirth within believers and by using prayer and study groups (called "conventicles") to awaken them to God. Spener and followers of the Pietist movement believed that a person's "inner light" (received at the "new birth" experience) should lead to a transformational process (called conversion), which produces a deep relationship with Christ, and is sustained by active involvement in the study of God's Word and the practice of Christian beliefs.

The impact of pietistic doctrine continued to be felt hundreds of years into the future because of people like Wesley, Catherine and William Booth (founders of the Salvation Army), and A. B. Simpson (founder of the Christian and Missionary Alliance). Many of today's contemporary devotional authors have been significantly affected by Pietist writings, who seek to create a "deeper life for followers of Christ." Authors such as E. M. Bounds, F. B. Meyer, George Müeller, Andrew Murray, Watchman Nee, Jessie Penn-Lewis, and A. W. Tozer to name a few.[14]

Some other character/spiritual formation contributors of today's church include such leaders as Donald Bloesch, John Piper, Larry Crabb, James Bryan Smith, Richard Foster, Kenneth Boa, Henri J. M. Nouwen, and Dallas Willard. These individuals represent some of the finest minds on the subject of transformation during the late twentieth and early twenty-first centuries. Their writings have no doubt helped many believers find their way out of the "dry places" of life and have inspired them to connect with God and the Holy Spirit in a special way. In particular, the contribution by Dallas Willard in his book, *The Divine Conspiracy*, presents a simplistic model for both character and spiritual formation by addressing four primary components necessary for spiritual growth. He calls it the "Golden

---

[14] Urban T. Holmes III, *A History of Christian Spirituality: An Analytical Introduction*. Harrisburg: Morehouse Publishing, 298–304.

Triangle of Spiritual Growth." The model presented by Willard has a combination of ingredients necessary for the transformation of a believer's life. He states,

> A picture of the factors involved in the transformation of our concretely embodied selves from inside (the "mind") out (behavior) can be conveyed by what I call "The Golden Triangle of Spiritual Growth." This image is designed to suggest the correlation in practical life of the factors that can certainly lead to the transformation of the inner self into Christ likeness.[15]

It is important that Willard understands the transformational process to be something that first takes place inwardly, then outwardly. A person's heart and mind must be impacted in such a way as to promote a strong desire to change their person or circumstances. This is achieved by combining the Holy Spirit, life events, utilizing spiritual disciplines, and by renewing someone's mind. He says,

> The intervention of the Holy Spirit is placed at the apex of the triangle to indicate its primacy in the entire process. The trials of daily life and our activities specially planned for transformation are placed at the bottom to indicate that where the transformation is actually carried out is in our real life, where we dwell with God and our neighbors. And at the level of real life, the role of what is imposed upon us ("trials") goes hand in hand with our choices as to what we will do with ourselves.[16]

---

[15] Dallas Willard, *The Divine Conspiracy: Rediscovering our Hidden Life in God.* San Francisco: Harper & Row, 1997, 347.

[16] Ibid, 347.

According to Willard, the Holy Spirit has the most important role to play in the transformational process after someone commits their life to Christ (John 3:5) because it is He who "continues to move upon and within us to enable us to do the kinds of works Jesus did (through 'gifts' of the Spirit) and to grow the kind of inward character that manifests itself in the 'fruit' or outcome of the Spirit" (Galatians 5:22–23).[17] The Holy Spirit alone will not transform a person's character; it takes the other components described in the "Golden Triangle" along with a willing response of the individual in need of transformation. The triangle's next component, the "ordinary events of life" is an insightful look at how God uses everyday circumstances to shape and form a believer's character. Trials and tribulations are said to be God's shaping tools, which present themselves as "temptations." Willard uses James 1:2–4 to validate this position, "My brethren, count it all joy when ye fall into divers temptations; knowing this, that the trying of your faith worketh patience. But let patience have her perfect work, that ye may be perfect and entire, wanting nothing" (KJV).

He along with Reggie McNeal, Robert Clinton and others believe that divine testing and life circumstances assist in the formation of Christlike character. Willard also embraces this truth when he cites Romans 5:1–5 as a support text for his argument, especially verses 3 and 4, "And not only so, but we glory in tribulations also: knowing that tribulation worketh patience; and patience, experience, and experience, hope" (KJV).

In order to grow "into the mind" of Jesus, we must accept the "trials" of ordinary existence as the place where we are to experience and find the reign of God with us as actual reality.[18] Willard believes that the book of Colossians contains the best overall statement of spiritual formation for a disciple of Christ in the New Testament. This is due to an emphasis on the actions of a believer, which is a major concern of this particular book. Being and doing are of

---

[17] Dallas Willard, *The Divine Conspiracy Rediscovering Our Hidden Life in God*, San Francisco: Harper & Row, Publishing, 1997 348.

[18] Ibid, 347.

great importance to the Apostle Paul in his writing to the church at Colossae. Therefore, Willard sees this epistle as a very important commentary on Christian character development and formation.

The third phase of Willard's "Golden Triangle" involves "planned disciplines to put on a new heart." Willard defines the word *discipline* as "any activity within our power that we engage in to enable us to do what we cannot do by direct effort."[19] He equates the word *discipline* to the word *practice*. He says, "Practice is discipline, but not all discipline is practice."[20] Therefore, he understands that in order for a person to be disciplined in anything, he must establish a life or practice so that they can perfect a skill or habit. Spiritual disciplines are disciplines designed to help someone become active and effective in the spiritual realm of their heart, and they are used to help us withdraw from dependence on human, natural or fleshly support.[21] Ultimately, we must learn to depend on God and His kingdom for support. As believers learn to follow Christ's example of spiritual disciplines such as "solitude, silence, study of scripture, prayer, and service to others,"[22] they too can experience spiritual fulfillment by practicing these and many others modeled throughout church history. The primary use for spiritual disciplines is to quiet our flesh and its activities in order to allow the Holy Spirit to transform believers from the inside out.

Finally, Dallas Willard's "Golden Triangle" has at its center the need for believers to capture the "mind of Christ" throughout the transformative process by adhering to scriptures like Philippians 2:12–15 and Romans 13:14. Both of these texts prioritize the need to quench the desires of the flesh by becoming more Christlike in word, actions, and deeds (see Philippians 2:12–15). Putting on the mind of Christ is foundational for the "Golden Triangle" process to work properly because the Scriptures and the Holy Spirit will work

---

[19] Dallas Willard, *The Divine Conspiracy Rediscovering Our Hidden Life in God*, San Francisco: Harper & Row, Publishing, 1997, 353.

[20] Ibid, 353.

[21] Ibid, 353.

[22] Ibid, 355.

together to perfect the heart (inner life) of a follower of Christ. Willard makes a powerful statement about his "Golden Triangle" model when he said, "In fact, all three points of the triangle are absolutely essential to one another as well as to the overall goal of spiritual growth. None will work on its own."[23]

When there is a balanced blending of each component of Willard's Triangle operating in someone's life, character/spiritual transformation can and will be achieved by anyone seeking to be changed for God and His kingdom. The model presented by Dallas Willard will serve as a foundational blueprint for the transformation of character and for the cultivation of values, which are consistent with the necessary components needed to shape a leader or follower of Jesus Christ. I have used Willard's model as a framework for the development of a "next generation" model. The next generation model will be as follows:

---

[23] Dallas Willard, *The Divine Conspiracy Rediscovering Our Hidden Life in God*, San Francisco: Harper & Row, Publishing, 1997, 349.

Values Transformation Diamond for Christlike Character

THE ACTION OF THE HOLY SPIRIT

(Provides the *Power* to change)

The power (grace) of the Holy Spirit (as the change agent) is now made available to us as He uses the other components to transform our lives.

CENTERED IN THE MIND OF CHRIST

(Holy Scriptures)

EVENTS OF LIFE

Trials and Tribulations
(Provides the *Examination*)

Trials and tribulations provide teachable moments and will allow for the examination of character while under pressure.

Centered in the Mind of Christ (Holy Scriptures)

Values transformation is founded upon a *biblical worldview*, which is cultivated by applying the Holy Scriptures to everyday life.

SPIRITUAL DISCIPLINES

(Provides the *Willingness* to change)

This component helps to prepare our heart and mind for change by making us willing to be transformed.

MENTORING/COACHING

(Provides *Accountability* during the process of change)

The mentor/coach is responsible for helping the protégé (student) to process everything that has happened or is happening in their life in order to help them maintain a balanced perspective throughout the values transformation process for character development. Accountability to standards, forms, and values are key with this component.

Figure 8. Values Transformation Diamond by Dr. Keith Attles, DMin.

The Values Transformation Diamond (VTD) of character development takes into account that character is formed by the synchronization of many variables into one harmonious process over an extended period of time. If any of the VTD components are missing during the formation process, it will no doubt limit the effectiveness of the transformation.

First, "The Action of the Holy Spirit" takes into account that the believer is willing to be changed by the power of God's Spirit. The presence of God works inwardly to strengthen, undo prior bondages (mental and emotional), release God's grace, convict of sin, and guide the individual in areas relating to decision-making, purposeful living, choice of values, and communication with God and others. If the Holy Spirit is allowed to do His work, the transformative power and ability will be available to change an individual. It is important to understand that the Holy Spirit works in conjunction with the other components detailed in the VTD. The second component called the "Events of Life: Trials and Tribulation" is where the Holy Spirit joins with the everyday events of life to refine someone's values, purify a heart, or produce an attitude of humility. This occurs because of the decisions a person makes, are outside of the purposes of God, or because it is a person's season to endure hardship that has been ordained by the Lord. In either case, the end result is to transform the believer into the likeness of Christ after having endured difficult circumstances (Philippians 2:5–11). Trials and tribulations have a way of producing the "fruit of the Spirit" (Galatians 5:22–23) in the believer's life, which is the character of Christ.

The third component, which is necessary for the VTD model, is "Centered in the Mind of Christ." This section sought to reveal how the scriptures (both Old and New Testaments) are vital to the transformation process because they create a biblical worldview that can now rival a person's preexistent value system (better known as theory conscience) for change to be possible. The Holy Spirit will always agree with the Scriptures when it comes to shaping a person's character, and He will also use the "events of life" to perform the needed inner-heart work associated with transformation. A Christian's beliefs, values, convictions, and character must be heavily influenced by God's values found only in the Holy Scriptures. Transformation can occur because there has been the "renewing of the mind" as set forth in Romans 12:2, which enable someone to "test" (prove) the new biblical value against their preexisting value system. If the Scriptures are understood and obeyed, the Holy Spirit is released to impart transformational power to the mind, and soon an overcomer of life's events will be born.

The fourth component in this model is "Spiritual Disciplines." These are practices that help the "flesh" (our physical body or evil desires) to become subservient to the Holy Spirit within the believer. Examples of these practices are fasting, prayer, silence, chastity, confession, and fellowship. According to Dallas Willard, the disciplines can be divided into two main groupings, *Disciplines of Abstinence* and *Disciplines of Engagement.* The combination of these groupings being practiced daily can produce a life more submitted to God, the Holy Spirit, and other people. A person's willful participation in the practice of spiritual disciplines, along with the Holy Spirit and the other components necessary for change, can yield the Christlikeness someone has been seeking in their walk with God.

The final component in the VTD model is that of the "Mentor/Coach." This much-needed individual can be used as a coordinator to assist in the understanding of what the believer/protégé is experiencing, as well as interpret current circumstances and to broaden perspective for the protégé. A protégé will also receive the benefit of accountability for their lifestyle choices and character deficiencies. With each of these components working together, a person's value system can definitely be influenced and their character transformed for the glory of God.

When comparing the models, the first generation Golden Triangle differs from the Values Transformation Diamond (VTD) because of one additional component, which is vital to the character formation process. The "Mentor/Coach" is the final component added to Willard's Golden Triangle because of the need for accountability during the entire transformational process. A mentor/coach is a highly skilled or trained individual who has committed himself to a relational experience in order to transfer resources of wisdom, information, experience, confidence, insight, status, etc. to empower a mentoree toward understood goals and objectives. A mentor or coach will perform similar roles and are there primarily to help shape an individual's life in some meaningful way. A major contribution these individuals play in the development of a mentoree is to assess, adjust, and train them in their pursuit for Christlike character.

The main objective of every component within the VTD is to develop the character of a mentoree over time to a place of maturity, effectiveness, and ultimately Christlikeness for service to God and others. The character of a person is literally the foundation for everything else that will follow throughout their life and ministry. If the foundation is faulty and weak, then the possibility for faulty and weak ministry will follow. If the foundation is strong and Christlike, then the possibilities for success are endless. Many of God's servants throughout the Bible had tremendous anointing but had faulty character, Samson, Saul, Gehazi, and Judas to name a few.

The anointing is tied to character! Someone may get away for many years operating under a powerful anointing, but eventually their deficiency of character qualities will eventually surface and usually ruin that individual's life and ministry.

Character and the Anointing
Character and Integrity

—— ❧ ——

I have often wondered what the connection between the anointing of God and character is. This question has compelled me to find an answer in the scriptures as well as life itself.

In order to adequately embrace the meaning of the term character, certain words like honesty, integrity, and virtue will be used synonymously throughout this chapter in order to build a complete picture and meaning for this word. Second, a broad definition of character will be analyzed so that a balanced interpretation of the word can be realized.

Therefore, character has been defined as:

1. the seat of one's moral being,
2. the inner life of a man,
3. what is displayed by the actions of an individual under pressure,
4. who we are and not what we have done,
5. what we do when no one is looking,
6. the combination of qualities distinguishing any person or class of persons,
7. not only that which other people see on the exterior but that which other people do not see, and
8. the sum total of the qualities, traits, and values that determine who a person is and how he or she will operate in their world.

According to Gordon MacDonald in his book, *When Men Think Private Thoughts,* he defined character as "the composite of a person that shows moral and spiritual structure in action."[24] MacDonald continued this train of thought by saying, "Character describes the inner soil out of which actions and words grow." Finally, he said, "Character might be noted as the collection of traits and behaviors that reflect the spiritual orientation (or its lack) of a man's life."[25] All of the insights into character given by MacDonald reveal that character involves inner traits, which manifest outwardly through speech and conduct (actions). He later concluded the definition of character by quoting eight insightful quotations by anonymous contributors. The most salient of these quotes is "character is defined by how a man relates to the weak and helpless."[26] This statement speaks volumes about the inner traits or core values which govern a person's decision of why and how they will treat someone weaker than themselves. Another noteworthy quotation by Elbert Hubbard, a turn-of-the-century American entrepreneur and philosopher (founder of Roycroft), said, "Many a man's reputation would not know his character if they met on the street."

All this points to one primary truth that character is an internal reality and quality that exhibits itself through outward manifestations. *Webster's Dictionary* defines character as "a distinctive quality...one of the attributes or features that make up and distinguish the individual...the complex of mental and ethical traits marking and often individualizing a person, group, or nation."[27] Perhaps the most profound and insightful definition ever given about character came from Frank Damazio when he said, "Character is the sum total of all negative and positive qualities in a person's life, exemplified by one's thoughts, values, motivations, attitudes, feelings and actions."[28]

---

[24] Gordon MacDonald, *When Men Think Private Thoughts* (Nashville: Thomas Nelson Publishers, Tennessee), 1997.

[25] Ibid, 190.

[26] Ibid, 198.

[27] *Webster's Ninth New Collegiate Dictionary,* s. v. "character."

[28] Frank Damazio, *The Making of a Leader* (Portland: Trilogy Productions, 1988), 106.

This definition encapsulates the inherent meaning of this word because it emphasizes the inner realities of (thoughts, attitudes, motivations) to reveal unseen characteristics, which influence a person's personality. Next, he showed how inner realities become outward expressions through actions governed by the core of one's being. He further addresses this topic by discussing how pressurized situations, relationships, and the workings of the Holy Spirit all work together to produce or reveal a person's true character.

For the purposes of this topic, it is important to draw a comparison between the words *integrity* and *character* due to the close association both words have to each other. According to *Webster's Dictionary*, integrity means: (1) an unimpaired condition, soundness; (2) firm adherence to a code of conduct, especially moral or artistic values, incorruptibility; and (3) the quality or state of being complete or undivided, completeness—synonym, see honesty."[29] Therefore, a person of character and integrity is a complete person who is undivided from the inside out of their personality and actions. John Maxwell stated that, "When I have integrity, my words and my deeds match up. I am who I am, no matter where I am or who I am with." He continued by saying, "People with integrity have nothing to hide and nothing to fear; their lives are an open book." V. Gilbert Beers, says, "A person of integrity is one who has established a system of values against which all of life is judged." Simply stated, "Integrity is not what we do as much as who we are."[30] Both words suggest that we are what we are because of what is at the core of our being, the product of a person's value system. Author Reggie McNeal gives more clarity to the topic of integrity when he sees it as a "character quality that permeates every area of a person's life."[31] In his opinion, integrity is a by-product of character, which cannot be hidden because it "permeates" or seeps through someone's life.

---

[29] *Webster's Ninth New Collegiate Dictionary*, s. v. "integrity."

[30] John C. Maxwell, *Developing the Leader Within You* (Nashville: Thomas Nelson Publishers, 1993), 35–37.

[31] Reggie McNeal, A *Work of Heart* (San Francisco: Jossey-Bass, 2000), 128.

In his book entitled, *Integrity*, Stephen Carter examined the many places within our society in need of integrity: philosophy, theology, history, and law, along with a host of other areas. Professor Carter defined integrity by using a three-step approach as follows: (1) discerning what is right and what is wrong, (2) acting on what you have discerned even at personal cost, and (3) saying openly that you are acting on your understanding of right from wrong. He explained each step by saying, "The first criterion captures the idea of integrity as requiring a degree of moral reflection. The second brings in the idea of an integral person as steadfast, which includes the sense of keeping commitments. The third reminds us that a person of integrity is unashamed of doing the right."[32] A person of integrity must search their soul in order to discern if what they believe is right or wrong based upon a previous set of established values and convictions. If a person can receive what they believe as truth, the author believes that this should cause someone to act in line with their belief system. Simply, they will take action by getting involved toward correcting a perceived wrong or injustice. Step three should lead someone to verbalize a particular conclusion resulting in an action. His definition of integrity begins with an inward journey that ends with outward action and verbalization; this is a person of integrity. Professor Carter saw the topic of integrity to be something that affects every phase of life and society, and if we continue to deny its importance, it may destroy our American utopia. This book, along with David Wells' *Losing Our Virtue*, are highly recommended for individuals concerned with the fate of people and society.

Besides Mac Donald, Maxwell, Carter and others, Aristotle, "the godfather of the philosophical discussion of character," was able to build on his Greek understanding of behaviors affecting people as a whole. Greeks believed that:

> Human beings are social creatures, human behavior can be shaped, certain behaviors are helpful for the society and the individual and

---

[32] Stephen L. Carter, *Integrity* (New York: Harper Collins, 1996), 7.

others harmful, the best way to identify good behavior is to look to a good role model, and that good behavior—the key to a good life—is most likely when those behaviors have become habits after years of repetition.[33]

THE PURSUIT OF CHARACTER

The Greeks saw good behavior as a virtue that included the idea of strength or the capacity to perform an act. Virtue was what you did, not what you did not do. Therefore, a person could be virtuous only through exercising virtues in daily acts, much like an athlete exercises their body for competition. This exercise was seen as the basis for forming character. The Greeks recognized four cardinal virtues: "Prudence (practical wisdom), justice (acts of fairness), courage (fortitude to face adversity), and temperance (self-discipline to control one's desires)."[34] In order for a person to exhibit virtue or character, he or she had to have all four qualities operating in her or his life simultaneously. The reason why was because Greeks believed that each core virtue made the others possible and the individual balanced in their approach to life.

Another important understanding of the word *character* for the Greeks can be found in the only scripture in the New Testament bearing its usage. Hebrews 1:3 uses "express image" for "character," metaphorically describing the Son of God as "the very image" (mark, the impression) of His substance. The Son of God is not merely His "image" or His "*character*," He is the "image" or impress of His substance or essence. The most basic meaning of the word denotes: (1) mark or stamp, made by engraving, etching, imprinting, branding (Revelation 13.16), and (2) by metonymy likeness, handiwork, the thing formed (Acts 17:29).[35] It can also mean a representation of

---

[33] Taylor, 31.

[34] Ibid, 31.

[35] Timothy Friberg, Barbara Friberg, Neva F. Miller, *Analytical Lexicon of the Greek New Testament*. (Grand Rapids: Baker Books, 2000), 406.

something. Frederick William Danker comments on the word *character* that can be defined as: (1) a mark or impression placed on an object—impress, reproduction, representation, trademark; (2) something produced as a representation, reproduction; (3) characteristic trait or manner, distinctive mark; and (4) an impression that is made, outward aspect, outward appearance, form.[36]

Both Greek definitions of the word *character* given by Friberg and Danker suggest that Jesus Christ is not only God's "image," but He is His substance or, better yet, His essence. Frank Damazio in his book, *The Making of a Leader,* understands the Greek meaning of character to be translated as "*image.*" He said that "character" is a noun derived from the word *charasso,* which means a notch, indentation, a sharpening, scratching or writing on stone, wood, or metal. This word came to mean an embosser and a stamp for making coins. In Hebrews 1:2, the writer stated that Christ is the very character of God, the very stamp of God's nature, and the one in whom God stamped or imprinted His being. Finally, the author concluded his definition by saying how our English word "*character* is said to be a distinctive mark impressed, or otherwise formed, by an outside (or internal) force upon an individual."[37]

Character then is the true essence of a person's life that manifests itself through outward forms of communication and action. Jesus Christ is the essence of His Father and the visible representation of His person as noted in Hebrews 1:3. It was literally the things Christ experienced that revealed His character and the life He led which provided proof that He was an "imprint or stamp" of God Himself.

Many of God's servants have been empowered (anointed) by the Holy Spirit but have failed to embrace the connection between character development and the anointing. If we were to examine the lives of some biblical characters such as Abraham, Jacob, Moses, David, or King Saul, it would become obvious of the importance

---

[36] Frederick Danker, William *A Greek-English Lexicon of the New Testament and Other Early Christian Literature 3rd Ed,* (Chicago: University of Chicago Press), 2000.

[37] Damazio, 107.

of both character and the anointing. The question we should ask is, why did it take so many years for each of these servants to step into the fullness of their ministry potential? The answer is simply that "God makes the man (character development) before He makes the ministry (a user of God's anointing). For example:

- Moses, forty years in the desert
- Joseph, thirteen years in prison
- David, thirteen years running from Saul
- Jesus, thirty years before beginning ministry
- Apostle Paul, three and a half years in an Arabian desert (Acts 9:1–9)

God uses character development strategies to refine a person's heart and motives, to conform them to his purposes through brokenness, negative and positive circumstances, the use of time, and even by promotion and blessings. The way in which the Lord deals with our character development is an endless list, but know that He can and will use anything during this shaping process.

It has been stated that a person's gift can exalt them to tremendous heights in life, but it is character that will keep them there. I have found this to be a very true statement because I have examined the lives of athletes, politicians, elite business people, everyday individuals, and especially God's servants throughout history. Here are a few individuals that we can glean truth from concerning character development, who also were highly anointed people. The first person we will examine is Joseph the son of Jacob, who had many brothers that envied him and were jealous of their father's favor toward him. Joseph had a prophetic dream ministry and a high business acumen that he used to exalt himself above his brothers on a daily basis. When Jacob gave Joseph the "coat of many colors," it served as a source of contention within the family, thus, causing division and many other problems. Joseph's main character flaw was pride, and the Lord knew that in order for him to fulfill his destiny, this had to be addressed. Joseph having been sold to the Midianites, Potiphar's wife's accusation, an unjust imprisonment, his disappointment with the lack of help from the butler and baker for his freedom, ultimately left him broken in heart and mind. This breaking process is absolutely necessary for anyone who will carry the anointing of the Holy Spirit. Total submission to the Lord is always a qualifying factor for how much of the anointing we will carry throughout our ministry. Joseph was able to accomplish his ministry purpose of preserving posterity because he endured the process of character development. Once we have been changed in heart and mind, we will be able to experience the power of forgiveness, live a life of true repentance, and see the result in the ongoing release of God's anointing.

The second person we will examine is Moses, the servant of God. This man's journey began with a life of privilege but soon became a life of dishonor, alienation, and isolation as he sought refuge in a desert location. Moses killed an Egyptian and thought that his secret would remain unknown, but the Lord used the situation as the beginning of a character development process. Moses would learn about brokenness, leadership, mercy, repentance, shepherding, warfare, project management, worship, communion with Jehovah, miracles, healing, salvation, and much more. All of these situations were designed to teach Moses how to depend on the Lord as opposed to himself, thus, transforming his character in the process. Moses had to have Egypt taken out of him before the Lord could use him to take his people out of Egypt. Brokenness is an integral part of God's process necessary for the individual to become an able carrier of His anointing of the Holy Spirit. I believe that the Lord's design for us in the New Testament is to have an equal balance of fruit and gifts. Nine gifts of the Holy Spirit (1 Corinthians 12:7–11) and nine fruits of the Spirit (Galatians 5:22–23) or if interpreted as nine gifts equals the grace of God expressed by His anointing versus nine fruit equals the character of God's love. To be a complete believer or minister of God, you must have a balance between

Power is the anointing (Isiah 61:1–3) and love is the character of God working within us.

Somehow if we are not able to fully understand the importance of this truth, we can examine the life of Samson. Detailed below is an analysis of Samson's life, especially as it pertains to his choices for life and ministry. Certain character flaws in Samson's life can be reviewed by doing a line by line evaluation of what ultimately led to his downfall as a leader.

The Life of Samson (Judges 14–16)

1. He desired an "non-Hebrew" wife of the Philistines (Judges 14:1–4).
2. He had a serious problem guarding his passion for women (Judges 14:11).
3. He entertained ungodly people throughout much of his life (Psalm 1:1–3, Judges 13:12–18).
4. He had anger issues (Judges 14:19).
5. He trusted in people who lacked integrity (Judges 15:1–2).
6. He used his anointing and talents on foolish pursuits (Judges 15:3–5).
7. He sought refuge "in the top of the rock Etam," instead of the Lord (Judges 15:7–11).
8. He desired the company of a harlot (Judges 16:1–3).
9. He loved a woman in the valley of Sorek named Delilah (Judges 16:4).
10. He allowed Delilah to entrap him and turn him over to his enemies, the Philistines (Judges 16:5–20).
11. He allowed his familiarity with the Lord to be his undoing. "I will shake myself, and he wist not that the Lord was departed from him" (Judges 16:20).
12. He dies as a result of his unrestrained lifestyle (Judges 16:21–31).

Samson's life should serve as a reminder of how unrestrained passions and unholy living can ultimately destroy a person's life and ministry. Character and the anointing are always unified in the eyes of the Lord and must be constantly monitored to ensure a life of purity and power and serve the Lord.

In the chapter entitled "Anointing the Unsanctified," a powerful truth found in Exodus 30:32 says, "Upon man's flesh shall it not be poured…" references the Holy Anointing Oil. Samson's character flaws and "fleshly" living should have disqualified him from ministering under God's anointing because the end result would be failed ministry. I have found that the Lord may use someone because of their availability and not because of them having character and integrity as their foundation. Samson's lust for women, pride, and unholy living eventually caught up to him in the end (as it always does) leaving him humiliated, imprisoned, and broken as a servant of God. Not only should we look at Samson but also the life of King Saul, Judas, and even Demas who had forsaken Paul in the ministry (2 Timothy 4:10). The process of character formation is usually a long intrusive journey into the heart and mind of a follower of Christ. Some believers and leaders alike believe that God's grace alone is enough to endure the challenges of life on the road ahead, but biblical evidence in both the Old and New Testaments does not totally support this position.

A true balance of character and the anointing is the difference maker in determining successful and unsuccessful ministry outcomes. One final recommendation I would like to make is when guidelines are established in the selection of people for ministry, there must be a requirement to have a history of stable, reliable character traits more than an anointing alone (Exodus 18:21–25, Micah 6:8, Acts 6:2–3, 1 Timothy 3:1–7, 1 Timothy 3:8–13, and 1 Timothy 4:6–16).

Frank Damazio in his book, The Making of a Leader, states, "Anointing oil was also used figuratively in the Bible to portray different character qualities that would receive the blessing of God." Christian leaders should see that God is interested in more than the personal development of the gifts of the Spirit, but more importantly, God wants to develop in them the fruit of the Spirit. As stated before in this book, God desires a balance between character (integrity) and anointing (power) in every leader's ministry. Listed below are some of the most important character qualities, which the Bible connects with receiving the anointing of the Spirit:

Concern. "Thou anointest my head (David, a shepherd concerned for the sheep's' welfare) with oil" (Psalm 23:5b).

Giving. "The liberal (giving) person shall be made fat (filled with oil)" (Proverbs 11:25).

Diligence. "The soul of the diligent shall be made fat (filled with oil)" Proverbs 13:4).

Trust. "He who trusts in the Lord shall prosper (be made fat with oil)" Proverbs 28:25).

Responsibility. "About this time tomorrow I will send you (Samuel) a man (Saul)…and you shall anoint him to be prince over my people Israel" (1 Samuel 9:16).

Righteousness. "Thou hast loved righteousness and hated iniquity, therefore God, even thy God, has anointed thee with the oil of gladness above thy fellows" (Psalm 45:7).

Purity. "Wash yourself, therefore, and anoint yourself (Ruth) and put on your best clothes and go down to the threshing floor" (Ruth 3:3).

Courage. "They (the enemy) set the table, they spread out the cloth, they eat, they drink; "Rise up, captains, oil the shields,' for thus saith the Lord to me, "Go station the sentry"" (Isaiah 21:5–6).

Obedience. "O mountains of Gilboa, let not dew nor rain be on you, nor fields of offerings. For the shield of the mighty was defiled, the field of Saul, not anointed with oil" (2 Samuel 1:21, 1 Samuel 15:22).

Submissiveness. "This is the law of the leper (a type of the sinner) in the day of his cleansing. Now he shall be brought in to the priest… then the priest shall take…the log of oil and present them as a wave offering before the Lord" (Leviticus 14:2, 12; see also oil in vs. 10, 14–18, 21, 24, 26–29).

Unity. "Behold how good and how pleasant it is for brothers to dwell together in unity! It is like the precious oil upon the head" (Psalm 133:1-2).

Joy. "The Spirit of the Lord God is upon me because the Lord has anointed me…to grant those who mourn in Zion…the oil of gladness" (Isaiah 61:3).

Humility and Brokenness. "And behold there was a woman in the city who was…standing behind Him at His feet, weeping…kissing His feet, and anointing them with the perfume" (Luke 7:36–50).

These are some of the most essential character qualities in a leader's life. With their development, a leader can believe God for a greater anointing.

RESOURCES

Keith Beasley-Topliffe, *The Upper Room Dictionary of Christian Spiritual Formation.* Nashville: Upper Room Books, 2003.

Frank Damazio, *The Making of a Leader.* Portland: City Christian Publishing, 1986.

Richard J. Foster, and James B. Smith. *Devotional Classics: Selected Readings for Individuals and Groups.*
San Francisco: Harper Collins, 2005, 55.

Kenneth O. Gangel, and James C. Wilhoit, *The Christian Educator's Handbook on Spiritual Formation.*
Grand Rapids: Baker Books, 1994, 22.

Urban T. Holmes III, *A History of Christian Spirituality: An Analytical Introduction.* Harrisburg: Morehouse
Publishing, 298–304.

T.L. Osborn, *Healing the Sick: A Living Classic,* Tulsa: Harrison House, 339–350.

Dallas Willard, *The Divine Conspiracy Rediscovering Our Hidden Life in God.* San Francisco: Harper & Row, Publishing, 1997, 349.

Testimonies of the Anointing's Power

In T. L Osborn's book, *Healing the Sick*, there are many stories which reference the power of God's anointing through healings and deliverance.

Jesus said, "These signs shall follow them that believe." Not the doubter but them that believe in the name, the name of Jesus. "They shall cast out devils, they shall speak with new tongues, they shall take up serpents, and if they drink any deadly thing, it shall not hurt them. They shall lay hands on the sick, and they shall recover."

Someone asked, "What does it mean to cast out devils?" It means that the man with the Holy Ghost dwelling in him is the master and has dominion over every devilish force and counterfeit.

As Johannesburg, some said, "Your power is hypnotism." One night, God demonstrated through us the falsity of that accusation. The power that is within the true Christian is the power of the Living Christ, and "greater is he that is within you, than he that is in the world" (1 John 4:4).

The following are testimonials from *Healing the Sick*.

THE POWER OF GOD AGAINST HYPNOTISM

In Johannesburg Tabernacle at a Sunday service about a year ago, God instantly healed a lame girl. She came from Germiston. She had been suffering for three and a half years from what doctors said was either an extreme case of rheumatism or the first stage of hip disease. She was not able to get up the steps without assistance when she came to the platform to be prayed for.

They asked her, "How long have you been sick?"

She said, "For three and a half years."

"Have the doctors treated you?"

"Yes, for two and a half years, and then they gave me up."

"Who has been treating you for the last year?"

"A hypnotist."

Just then, a well-known hypnotist arose in the audience, moved forward, and took a front seat.

The leader said, "Never mind the hypnotist, Jesus is going to heal you right now. In two minutes, you will be well."

They laid hands on her and prayed, and instantly, the Lord delivered her, and she walked up and down the platform several times to demonstrate to herself and the audience that she was well.

I stepped back and looked at her, my heart going out in praise to God for His mercy when suddenly the Spirit of the Lord descended upon me in power, not in any gentle influence but with a mighty intense power, a spirit of revulsion against the spirit of the hypnotist.

I stepped on the platform directly in front of him and said, "Are you the man who has been hypnotizing this woman?"

He replied, "Yes, I am." He rose to his feet and looked toward me in a challenging attitude.

I said to him, "In the name of Jesus Christ, you will never hypnotize anybody again."

And before I realized what I was doing. I reached over the front of the platform, grasped his collar with my left hand, while with my right, I slapped him on the back, saying "In the name of Jesus Christ, the Son of God, you come out of him."

He laughed at me and said, "Do you mean to tell me that I cannot hypnotize anybody?"

I said, "Yes, sir, that is the end of that thing. The devil that caused you to hypnotize people is out."

He worked all night in an endeavor to hypnotize some subjects, and in the morning at six came to my house, saying, "This is a might serious business, mister, this is my bread and butter."

He wanted me to give him back the power to hypnotize. I explained to him that it was not I but Jesus who cast out the devil.

I added, "Brother, it looks to me as if the Lord wanted you to earn an honest living."

He cancelled his engagement at the theater where he was billed to give exhibitions, and the last heard of, he was working in a mine and earning an honest living. That demonstrated that there is a mighty manifestation of the spirit of God that has dominion over every other power. It is still true that in His name, we shall cast out devils.

RAISED FROM THE DEAD
1104 BROADWAY, INDIANAPOLIS

About five weeks ago, one Sunday night, I was attending the meeting and was sitting listening to Sister Etter preaching when I turned real sick, and a voice said to me, "Come with me." I went outside the church a sister accompanying me, and the same voice said again, "This is death, come now, go with me."

That was the last I remembered on earth, only I thought of my son in the army, and that no one would know where to send (inform him) to notify him of my death.

Presently, it seemed to me I was in heaven, in a place where there was such light and rest and joy. I heard singing and all kinds of different instruments.

I saw my earthly father and children and talked with the Lord, and then a voice said, "You can go back for a while," and then I heard Sister Etter's voice calling on me in the name of the Lord.

"Mrs. Sarah Nelson," Sr. Woodworth-Etter said.

On that occasion, there was a commotion, people going out to help and some coming back.

She asked, "What is the matter?"

As they did not wish to alarm the audience, they said, "She has fainted."

Sister Etter said, "She is all right, and even if the Lord should take her, she is ready. I wish the rest of you were as well prepared."

After quite a while, they carried her body in and said, "She is dead! The pulse has ceased to beat."

There was no motion of the heart, the body was cold and limp, and the face that of a corpse. Sister Etter gathered the others around her and spoke of Jesus being the resurrection and the life and prayed and called on her in the name of the Lord, and she opened her eyes.

When she opened her eyes, they were yellow, and she did not seem to know anything at first but sat in a big armchair, looking like a corpse. Later on in the meeting, she expressed a desire to testify, which she did. She has been attending meetings ever since and working daily.

HEALINGS ABOUND

After several other missions, we went to Springfield, Illinois, pitched our tents in Oak Ridge Park, and commenced a union meeting to build up the temple of our God. We made the call for all ministers and Christian workers to come up to the house of the Lord. Not one of the city preachers responded to the call except the Lutherans, several of whom came to the front. We were not acquainted with one person in the city.

The voice of God said, "I will be with you."

We lived in our tents, hired a cook, and paid all expenses, trusting God to provide all needful help. The first few days, the weather was very wet, and everything was against us. Although there were but eighteen persons present the first night, we shouted victory and told them that God was going to shake the city. The interest increased until there were thousands present. The altar was crowded day and night. They came from different states and all parts of the country to be healed of all manner of diseases. They were brought on beds, in cars, in chairs, on crutches, and in cabs, hundreds being healed and converted. There were three that we know of who were brightly converted and died before the meeting closed—a young lady and an old man nearly eighty years of age, another, an old man, saved at his home on his deathbed. Others were converted at their homes and some in the woods.

A little girl was carried into the meetings in her mother's arms. She was as helpless as a babe two days old. She had spinal meningitis, was paralyzed all over, her brain was impaired, her head dropped on her breast, and she had no use of her limbs. She had been sick for six months. For four months, she had not eaten anything but a little milk. I laid my hands on her commanded the unclean spirits to come out of her. In five minutes, she could sit up straight and raise her arms above her head. In five minutes, more she could talk and rose upon her feet, stepped up on the high altar, walked with her mother to the streetcars, went home, and could eat anything she wanted.

The next morning, she was the first one up, running from house to house, telling what God had done for her. It shook the whole neighborhood. This child could not exercise faith and did not seem to know what we were doing. Several children were wonderfully healed and also several infants. One little boy was healed of dropsy, stomach, and bowel trouble. His clothes could not be buttoned because he was so badly swollen. The swelling went down at once; his mother fastened every button on his vest and clothes and stood him on the platform where everyone could see what God had done. The little fellow said in a clear ringing voice that God had made him well.

JANUARY 15, 1951
CAMAGUEY, CUBA

The service was attended by great throngs of people. After the message, over 1,500 accepted Christ. Then the mass prayer was offered for the healing of the sick, and God surely answered from heaven.

One man who was blind from birth was led to the meeting, and as he listened to the message, he fell to the ground, having seen the Lord Jesus in a vision. He lay there for some time, and those around him thought he had died. Suddenly, he seemed to regain consciousness and stood to his feet with an expression of joy on his face, declaring, "I have seen the Lord, and now I see! I was blind, but now I see!" His sight was restored; he could see fine print. The multitude was hysterical with joy when they heard this report. Six deaf-mutes were healed during this service, one of which was fifty-five years of age and had been born in this condition. One young man, who was going to commit suicide, was gloriously converted. Several hernias, growths, and various classes of sickness and paralysis were instantly healed. To God be all the praise!

FEBRUARY, 10, 1953
GUATEMALA CITY, GUATEMALA

After the meeting last night, a woman who had been sitting in a car, crippled and unable to walk for over five years due to a broken spine, continued praying and suddenly felt that she should walk. She got out of her car and was made whole! Many witnessed the miracle.

Many thousands were present in the hot afternoon service. At least 2,500 accepted Christ in tears. Then I prayed for all who were sick. The miracle power of God filled the hillside.

The first woman to testify hadn't walked in fifteen years without two crutches. She was made whole and left her crutches. Then a lady of eighteen years was healed. She had tuberculosis in her hip, could not bend it, and had to walk with a crutch. She was completely healed and testified, weeping.

Then a young doctor came to the microphone to confirm her testimony, saying, "I know her. She was incurable. We treated her. She could not walk. It is true! We can only say truly God heals!"

Then a child who had polio was healed. An old man who had walked with a cane was restored after having suffered for twenty years. A woman whose foot was wrapped in cloth because of a cancerous ulcer was healed. The leg had been badly swollen, and she walked on crutches, but she was totally and miraculously restored. It was great!

A wealthy lady and her son came running, extremely excited. He fell on my neck weeping, crying out, "Oh, Mr. Osborn, here's my mother. She has been deaf since my birth. She has never heard in twenty-three years. Now she is healed! She hears! Oh, He is so good!" Many people knew her. She testified in tears of joy.

Next was an old medical doctor who had not been able to walk for several years; he was restored. A woman who had a rupture for twenty years was healed. A policeman was healed. An old woman who was carried in arms to the meeting was made whole. A man who was brought in a wheelchair arose and walked, healed by God's power. A woman also was healed from her wheelchair. Afterward, over one thousand people remained in the audience who declared that they were healed, but we did not have time for their testimonies.

The night service was twice as large, and thousands more received Christ. Amongst a great host of miracles of healing was a boy who had been cross-eyed from birth. He was perfectly healed. A fine educated young football player from Honduras was healed of epilepsy. For twelve years, he had suffered convulsions, but tonight, he received Christ. He said that when the prayer for healing was prayed, he actually felt the strange evil power leave him like a whirling wind, then peace and freedom came to him. He wept and wept as he testified.

JULY, 4, 1954
JAKARTA, JAVA, INDONESIA

Thirty-thousand to forty-thousand people were jammed together on the "Lapangan Bantang" grounds in the capital city. I preached on the gospel for everyone, stressing John 3:16 and Psalm 103:3. The people are so hungry and eager to learn. Actually, it exceeds what we saw in Latin America. Fully eight thousand people raised eager hands to accept Jesus Christ into their hearts and pledged their lives to Him. This sounds fantastic, but it looks even more awesome, especially realizing that Java is 95 percent Muslim.

When we prayed for the sick, truly Christ confirmed His word. A boy who had been blind in both eyes was wonderfully healed and could see everything. A woman who had been blind in one eye for nine years was healed. A Chinese woman who had been crippled for twelve years and who could only hobble on two canes was miraculously healed. A woman who had been severely paralyzed on one side became perfect. She was so bad that her left side had been hard and stiff and drawn. Her arm had been drawn to her side, and her leg drawn and stiff. Every part of her body was healed. For eight years, she had not walked. Another woman who had been paralyzed on one side for nine years was completely restored.

Four men testified of how they had been cripples and were healed. One had not walked in over four years. At least eight or ten totally deaf people were healed. A woman whose shoulder had been broken and who had been unable to raise her arm for years was healed.

A great miracle was wrought on a little girl who had been the victim of a disease (probably polio), which had destroyed the strength and muscles in her legs. Her little legs and hips were just skin and bones, limp and useless. For over two years, the child had not taken a step. The father brought her and laid her in a rickshaw during our sermon, and she fell asleep. As I prayed for the sick, the father laid his hands on his child and prayed earnestly.

The child awoke and cried out, "Papa, I'm healed!" She was instantly made perfect. She walked and ran, perfectly normal. One could hardly believe she had ever been crippled, but many witnesses knew her. How we thanked God for His mercy!

Two lepers were cleansed; one had been a leper for five years and the other for twelve years. Both testified that every feeling was returned to the previously dead parts of their flesh. Oh, how they wept as they told what Jesus had done for them, and they promised to follow Him.

What Is the Anointing?

—— ∽ ——

There are many different definitions of the word *anointing* such as:

1. "The anointing of the Holy Spirit is when the Spirit is poured out upon a person for the purpose of empowering them to fulfill the ministry they have been called to. The anointing enables any minister in the Christian Church to deliver life to others" (Robert L).
2. "The anointing is a divine enablement for us to accomplish God's purposes on earth" (Denver Cheddie).
3. "What is the anointing? It is the power of God" (Benny Hinn).
4. "The anointing is 'the power of the Holy Spirit'" (Lori Wilke).

After having considered the definitions of what the anointing is believed to be, I would like to propose my personal understanding and definition of what the anointing is: "The anointing is the *consecrating* [setting apart] of *a vessel* [any object or person] through *the empowerment of the Holy Spirit for God's specific use or purpose*" (Keith Attles).

I believe this definition of the anointing is what the Scriptures and biblical words convey. Therefore, this definition will be analyzed by breaking it down into four separate categories. First, the act of anointing people or vessels can be evidenced by the account of God's calling and anointing of Aaron and his sons for the priestly office (Exodus 29–30). This is where God says that Aaron and his sons are

54

called, anointed, and appointed to "minister unto me in the priest's office" (Exodus 29:1, 29:30; "consecrated," Exodus 28:1, 3, 4, 41; Exodus 40:13, 15). The idea God was trying to convey with these instructors was that Aaron and his sons would minister to Him on behalf of the people. They were essentially mediators between God and man. The command to sanctify or consecrate them for the priesthood was God's way of saying "these individuals have been 'set apart' for divine business. They are not yours but mine." From the ceremonial washing (cleansing) to the priestly attire (Exodus 28:31–43), to the actual pouring of the holy anointing oil upon Aaron and his sons (Exodus 29:30, Psalm 133:2), it was a witness to the rest of the tribes of Israel that these individuals were "*set apart*" (from the rest) for his use and calling. Another important point included in my definition was that the anointing (oil) was to be poured upon animate or inanimate objects, which God chose to "*set apart*" (consecrated, sanctified). Exodus 30:26–30 supports this claim by showing how "vessels" (inanimate objects) in verses 26–28 were anointed with holy oil for use within the tabernacle of Moses, and verse 30 (animate objects), Aaron and his sons were anointed for service within and without the tabernacle (the inner and outer courts).

The next component found in the definition is that of the "*empowerment of the Holy Spirit*," which is the result of the act of pouring the holy anointing oil upon an object or person. Throughout the Bible, oil has always been understood to be a symbol of the Holy Spirit's presence (1 Samuel 16:13, Isaiah 61:1, Luke 4:18, Acts 10:38, 2 Corinthians 1:21–22, [1 John 2:20 "unction" is unguent or *smearing*, endowment is equals to anointing]). The coming of the Spirit upon someone or something was, in fact, the "anointing oil" being poured out by the Lord to indicate a "setting aside" for ministry purposes. When the "spirit of the Lord" came upon Samson (Judges 13:25), David (1 Samuel 16:13), Azariah (2 Chronicles 15:1), and Jesus (Luke 4:18–19, Matthew 3:16), they were recognized as having been empowered by the Lord for service in the ministry. A classic example of this truth can be evidenced in the life of Samson, who was raised up by the Lord to be a judge/deliverer of Israel, along with many others. Samson was a child of promise (Judges 13:2–3) because of the barrenness of his mother during the time of the Philistines' domination of Israel. An angel of the Lord appeared to Manoah and his wife and said unto her, "Behold now, thou art barren, and barest not: but thou shalt conceive, and bear a son." Now this was a conditional promise based on the parent's obedience to these conditions:

1. Drink no wine or strong drink
2. Eat no unclean thing
3. "No razor shall come upon his head: for the child shall be a Nazarite unto God from the womb:
4. He shall begin to deliver Israel out of the hand of the Philistines." (Judges 13:4–5)

The couple agreed to the terms of the vow and later conceived a son who grew under the blessing of the Lord (Judges 13:24). Now in Judges 13:25, the text says, *And the Spirit of the Lord began to move him at times in the camp of Dan between Zorah and Eshtaol.*

The spirit of the Lord is the anointing, which empowers and sets apart God's servants for the task at hand. Samson was to always be in a position of readiness as the spirit of the Lord (or the anointing) "moved" (pâ'am—to tap, beat regularly: hence, to impel or agitate, move, trouble) upon Samson in order to stir him from a place of rest into divine service or action. It was the troubling or agitating of the Spirit, which compelled Samson to allow the anointing to operate through him to impact others on God's behalf. Judges 14:6, 19 and 15:14 records how the Lord used Samson to do unusual feats of strength because the presence of the spirit of the Lord anointed him.

It is important to see how Samson was first "set apart" for divine use as a *vessel* of the Lord (Judges 13:4–5); and second, he was *empowered* by the spirit of the Lord for a *specific use and purpose* ("to deliver Israel out of the hand of the Philistines" [Judges 13:5]). All four components of my definition are present here and can be found in other places throughout the Bible, where God used people to operate under His anointing, as the calling of David to be king over Israel is further evidence of this truth. He was called by the Lord and anointed the first time by the prophet Samuel (1 Samuel

16:13). A second and third anointing on David's life happened in 2 Samuel 2:4 and 2 Samuel 5:3, but the actual "setting apart" occurred in 1 Samuel 16:13 (David was set apart from his brothers) and 1 Samuel 18:1–2 (David leaves his father's house and is "set apart" for his future training in the house of Saul). David as a *vessel* of the Lord is chosen (and inspected) by him to eventually be made the king of Israel (1 Samuel 16:1–3). Therefore, the third component of my definition is evidenced by the prophet Samuel anointing (sûk) David in a ceremony involving the "poured out" oil on him demonstrating the *empowerment* for service. The supernatural enablement he received was confirmed during his battle with Goliath in 2 Samuel 17:1–54 as he worked with the Holy Spirit's ability to win the battle. Ultimately, the Lord used David to be king over all Israel, thus bringing blessing, prosperity, unity amongst the tribes, and spiritual leadership to the covenant community. The Lord's *specific use and purpose* for His anointed vessel was finally realized; hence, completing the fourth component of the definition. I believe it becomes easier and easier to see the validity of this definition if we were to look for these components in the lives of God's other servants like Moses, Aaron, Elisha, Paul, and most definitely Jesus.

Next, we must see the components of the definition in Jesus's life and ministry as well. He was *consecrated ("set apart")*.

- Hebrew 10:5 (He was "set apart" to come from heaven to earth)
- John 1:14, 18 (He was "set apart" as God's only "begotten Son" [John 3:16])
- Hebrew 2:17 (He was "set apart" as our High Priest [Hebrew 3:1, 4:14, 5:8–10, 6:20, 8:1, 9:11])
- Acts 4:12 (He was "set apart" from all other holy men because He was and is the Savior of humanity)
- Luke 4:18, Acts 10:38 (He was "set apart" as the "Anointed One," "the Christ or the Messiah")

Here are just a few examples found in scripture, which show how Jesus Christ was "set apart" as an anointed servant of the Lord.

Jesus can also be looked at as a *vessel*, which was "set apart" for God's use. The word *vessel* can be defined in *Webster's Dictionary* as: (1) a utensil for holding something, as a bowl, pitcher, kettle, etc.; and (2) a person thought of being the receiver or repository of some spirit, influence, etc.

In my original definition of the term *anointing*, it is said that a vessel could be an "object or person." *Webster's Dictionary* supports this idea and clearly shows in the above definitions.

1. *Christ symbolically as an object*
   - Numbers 21:9, *Brazen Serpent*—the serpent on a pole is a type of Christ on the cross and all who look at him shall live.
   - Isaiah 4:2, Zechariahs 3:8, *Branch of the Lord*—Jesus is an extended branch to the drowning masses of humanity.
   - John 6:51–58, *Bread of God*—Bread is the main staple at every meal in every culture and provides sufficient nutrition to sustain body life.
   - Ephesians 2:20, the *Corner Stone*—it is the first and principal stone that unites the parts of the building together. Jesus the "rock" or "stone" is mentioned throughout scripture (Exodus 17:6, 33:21–22; Numbers 20:8–9; Daniel 2:31–45; 1 Corinthians 10:4; 1 Peter. 2:8).

2. *Christ symbolically as a person*
   - 1 John 2:1, the *Advocate*—one who pleads for another in a court of justice. In the case of Christ, He pleads our justification in the face of sin.
   - Hebrew 3:1, 6:20, *High Priest*—he was the chief among the priesthood, who was responsible for offering sacrifices to the Lord on mankind's behalf.
   - Daniel 9:25, *Messiah the Prince* also known as the Prince of peace in Isaiah 9:6. The Messiah would be an heir to the throne of God and ruler over God's creation (Colossians 1:13–20; Philippians 2:5–11;

Hebrew 1:1–2; Revelation 5:6, 7:9–10, 17; Acts 3:15, 5:31; and Revelation 1:5).

- Matthew 3:17, John 3:16, the *Son of God*—this title testifies to the fact that Jesus has the same nature and attributes of God in word, deed, and truth.

Jesus's *empowerment* by the anointing of the Holy Spirit was noted in both testaments (Isaiah 11:2, 61:1; Luke 4:18–20; Matthew 3:13–17; and Acts 10:38) and should be noted as His source of strength, power, and wisdom for service to God. Jesus Christ was the Messiah the Old Testament prophets declared would come (Psalm 2:2 with Acts 4:26, Daniel 9:25–26). Israel and other nations awaited His coming (John 1:41, Acts 2:36—"both Lord and Christ," that is "Sovereign and Messiah." John 4:25 and Acts 3:20, 5:42. Read the account of the wise men and Herod in Matthew 2:1–12 because they knew Jesus was the promised Messiah/Christ).

(Note: the English word *Christ* transliterates to the Greek "*christos*," meaning "anointed one," which translates the Old Testament word "*māšîaḥ*," transliterated "messiah," and means the "anointed one").

The *Theological Wordbook* states, "The term came to be applied to the coming King from the throne of David, the Messiah, who will one day rule over the restored Davidic kingdom."

Jesus was the "Anointed One" or "Messiah" who was empowered by the Holy Spirit (Isaiah 61:1 and Luke 4:18) to preach, heal, and deliver those who were held captive by the kingdom of darkness (Acts 10:38). This empowerment occurred when Jesus's cousin, John the Baptist, baptized Him in the Jordan River (Matthew 3:13–17), where the Holy Spirit "anointed" Christ for service to God. As a result, Jesus did many healings and miracles that confirmed His having been anointed by God as He sought to preach the "kingdom of God" message to the multitudes.

And Jesus went about all Galilee, teaching in their synagogues, and preaching the gospel of the kingdom, and healing all manner of sickness and all manner of disease among the people. And his

> *fame went throughout all Syria: and they brought*
> *unto him all sick people that were taken with divers*
> *diseases and torments, and those which were pos-*
> *sessed with devils, and those which were lunatic and*
> *those that had the palsy; and he healed them. And*
> *there followed him great multitudes of people from*
> *Galilee, and from Decapolis, and from Jerusalem,*
> *and from Judea, and from beyond Jordan. (Matthew*
> *4:23–25)*

There are a number of other scriptures that reveal the impact of the anointing in Christ's life through healings and miracles:

- Stilling the storm, Matthew 8:23, Mark 4:35
- A Hemorrhaging Woman, Matthew 9:20
- Walking on the sea, Matthew 14:25
- Feeding five thousand, Matthew 14:13
- Raising the woman's son, Luke 7:11
- Healing the man born blind, John 9:1
- Healing the two blind men, Matthew 9:27
- Cleansing a leper, Luke 5:12
- Raising Lazarus, John 11:43
- Turning water into wine, John 2:1

Each of these demonstrates the impact of the anointing of the Holy Spirit upon Jesus's ministry and is further proof of the transformative power of God that empowered Him for service.

Finally, we should examine the components of this definition by taking a serious look at the Church. The Greek meaning of the term "*church*" (*ekklesia*) is: (1) a regularly summoned legislative body, assembly; (2) a casual gathering of people, an assemblage, gathering; (3) people with shared belief, community, congregation, or simply the "called-out" ones. This is evident because of the breakdown of the words *ek*, *out of*, and kaleo, to call, the combination of two Greek words. One of the hidden meanings of the word *Church* is that of "calling out" a people to be "set apart" (consecrated/holy) unto the Lord. First Peter 2:9 says, "*But ye are a chosen generation, a royal priesthood, and holy nation, a peculiar people; that ye should shew forth the praises of him who hath called you out of darkness into his marvelous light.*"

God's church (*ekklesia*) has been "called out" of the world system (kingdom of darkness) and called to the kingdom of light in order for us to be "set apart" for service. Another title the church is called to be is a "holy nation," thus signifying its responsibility to be exclusively for God's use. The Greek word for "holy" used in the verse above is "*hagios,*" which means "sacred, pure, blameless, consecrated, most holy, saint." It can also mean "holy, set apart, sanctified, or consecrated. Its fundamental ideas are separation, consecration, devotion to God, and sharing in God's purity and abstaining from the earth's defilement" (Luke 9:26, 2 Peter 1:18). The Church (*ekklesia*) is to be pure and "set apart" in order to receive the fullness of God's blessing and power through the anointing of the Holy Spirit. The Church is to be holy because

1. *it is separated from the world* (John 15:19, 17:14–16, and 2 Corinthians 6:17),
2. *it is cleansed from sin* (Ephesians 5:26, 2 Corinthians 7:1, 1 Thessalonians 5:23–24, Hebrew 13:12, 1 John 1:7–9), and
3. *it is consecrated unto God* (Colossians 1:22, James 4:7, Romans 12:1, Ephesians 5:27).

The Church will one day realize its full potential as the "bride of Christ" (Ephesians 5:22–27, Revelation 19:6–9) when it embraces its call to holiness, purity, and faithfulness to Christ.

We have already discovered how the anointing oil could be applied to an object or person, but now we must understand how the church as God's vessel has been anointed by the Holy Spirit. First, we must comprehend the fact that Christ's Church is not an object (such as a building with stained glass, chairs, and a pulpit) but a living, breathing organism called his "body" (Romans 12:5; 1 Corinthians 10:16, 12:12, 12:27; Ephesians 4:12; Ephesians 5:23). Perhaps this is what Stephen meant when he called Israel the "church in the wilderness" (Acts 7:38). He realized that the Israelites were the original "called out ones" as a body of assembled people to the Lord. The children of Israel were not objects but a body of believers, which Stephen recognized as the "*ekklesia*" of the Old Testament. The New Testament Church is, in fact, a living assemblage of people who have been redeemed by Jesus Christ for the purpose of becoming a vessel through which the anointing (Holy Spirit) can flow.

The empowerment of Jesus for ministry service was recorded in Matthew 3:16, "*And Jesus, when he was baptized, went up straightway out of the water: and, lo, the heavens were opened unto him, and he saw the Spirit of God descending like a dove, and lighting upon him.*"

This factual event of Jesus's anointing is recorded for all to be appreciated. Before this empowerment took place, Bible history never records Jesus doing one healing or miracle prior to his being anointed by the Holy Spirit (Isaiah 61:1, Luke 4:18). This example was to serve as a model for future disciples of Christ, who joined in community to be called the Church. People who are in the Church are believed to be followers of the Christ and have been give the name "Christians," little anointed ones (Acts 11:26). Therefore, believers have always been expected by Jesus to be seekers of the anointing, which comes by the empowerment of the Holy Spirit (Matthew 10:1, Luke 10:1, 17–20, John 20:19–22, Mark 16:14–20, Acts 2:1–4, Acts 1:8). All of these texts suggest a supernatural enablement to do the work of God effectively and efficiently as believers receive their *empowerment* for service as did Christ.

Jesus gave a command to his disciples to wait and expect this empowerment (anointing) in Luke 24:49, "*And, behold, I send the promise of my Father upon you: but tarry ye in the city of Jerusalem, until you be endued with power from on high.*"

This states that there would be an *empowerment* (of the Holy Spirit) from heaven ("from on high") that was promised by Jesus in John 14:15–20 and John 16:7. The literal fulfillment of this promise manifested in Acts 2:1–4,

And when the day of Pentecost was fully come,
they were all with one accord in one place. And sud-

denly there came a sound from heaven as of a rush-
ing mighty wind, and it filled the house where they
were sitting. And there appeared unto them cloven
tongues like as of fire, and it sat upon each of them.
And they were all filled with the Holy Ghost, and
began to speak with other tongues, as the Spirit gave
them utterance.

Where the early disciples of Jesus received the baptism of the Holy Spirit on the day of Pentecost, Christ's same spirit now "came upon" them and dwelt within His believers empowering them for service to be His witnesses in all the world (Romans 8:11, 1 John 2:20, Acts 1:8). Thus, the plan of God through Christ was complete; His spirit could now be given again to "fallen" (Genesis 3:1–24) man after being "born again" through the work of the Christ (John 3:16, Acts 2:38, Ephesians 1:1–14). Jesus's expectation for the Church is to fully operate in a powerful anointing provided by the Holy Spirit, to undo the ravages of sin and the powers of darkness as stated in Mark 16:15–18,

And He said unto them, Go ye into all the
world, and preach the gospel to every creature. He
that believeth and is baptized shall be saved; but
He that believeth not shall be damned. And these
signs shall follow them that believe. In My name
shall they cast out devils. They shall speak with new
tongues. They shall take up serpents, and it they
drink any deadly thing, it shall not hurt them. They
shall lay hands on the sick, and they shall recover.

The presence of the anointing of the Holy Spirit will be evidenced by mighty acts of goodness, supporting the kingdom message of hope and deliverance to all who believe in Jesus as Lord and Savior. The anointing is Christ's gift for the Church to help us fulfill the Great Commission (Matthew 28:18–20) by reproducing mighty deeds. When will we utilize the fullness of Christ and stop relying on our own works to win the lost?

The final component of this definition, which impacts the Church's ability to do the work of Christ under the anointing, is that of being "set apart" for God's specific use or purpose. Every believer has been called by God to fulfill a specific purpose in His kingdom and is expected to accomplish a divinely assigned mission (Ephesians 1:3–5, 11, Romans 8:28–30, Ephesians 4:1). Just as Jesus called (or chose) the twelve to "become" His disciples, so the Lord has chosen us before the foundation of the world to be His servants. This means that the Lord has gifted and graced us to be partakers of His anointing so we would bring glory and honor to His name. This is made possible by the empowerment of the Holy Spirit (Isaiah 61:1, Zechariah 4:6, John 16:13, Romans 8:26, 1 Corinthians 2:10). The anointing of God's Spirit upon many of His servants is what made them able to hear, receive, and complete the will of God in their earthly ministries. People like Moses, Samson, Deborah (Judges 4:4), David, Jeremiah, and Paul along with many others are prime examples.

Therefore, the Church has received the indwelling anointing that was given to complete Christ's Great Commission at the beginning of its history (Acts 1:8, 2:1–4). If the early church needed the anointing of the Holy Spirit to extend God's kingdom throughout the earth, how much more does the twenty-first-century church need His help and guidance (Matthew 4:1, Acts 4:8, 31, 6:3, 8:38–39, 9:17–18, 11: 1–16, 13:1–3, 4–12, 19:1–7, 11–12, 20:24–27, 21:1–4, 28:1–10).

The significance of the definition is that it goes far beyond most surface definitions of the anointing and seeks to reveal major components, which help to illustrate the seriousness of this supernatural endowment. Many believers have not sought to understand God's commitment to those He has chosen to represent His kingdom with power and might.

Anointed for Service

The presence of the Lord has always been given to people in service to Him through the act of anointing with oil. There were three primary offices, which the Lord designated as special, requiring the servant to be "set apart" for divine service. The first was the office of the *prophet* (1 Samuel 19:16), *king* (1 Samuel 15:1, 16:1, 1 Kings 1:34) and *priest* (Exodus 28:41, 29:7). The prophet was responsible for the ministry of the Word of the Lord through prophecy; the priest had a ministry of reconciliation (Leviticus 8:1–13, 21:12, Exodus 30:20), and the king had the ministry of ruling and reigning over God's people. In Kevin Conner's book entitled *The Tabernacle of David*, he makes tremendous sense of this truth by saying, "A consideration of David's life story shows him to have touched these three offices of prophet, king, and priest.

1. David as prophet, the first anointing
2. David as king, the second anointing
3. David as priest, the third anointing

Another interesting truth, which can be extracted from the process of anointing with oil and the life of David, is that the different Hebrew words for "anoint" reveal a progression of divine enablement. The Hebrew words *cûwk* and *māshach* yield a progressive understanding of God's process in the life of His servant, David. *Cûwk māshachmāshach*, "to pour out," "to smear," and "to rub in."

David's being anointed three times point to a hidden truth about how the anointing grows (or increases) in our lives as we continue to mature during the process of having been initially anointed. David's three anointings:

First Anointing	Second Anointing	Third Anointing
"Poured out" (1 Samuel 16:13)	"Smeared in" (2 Samuel 2:4)	"Rubbed in" (2 Samuel 5:3)
He was set apart from his brothers.	He was made king over Judah.	He became king over Israel.
He killed a lion, bear, and a giant.	He became a leader of praise (Judah) and worship.	Israel means "he wrestled with God" or "God rules," the final stage in God's process.

What we can learn from the chart above is that like David, we must endure what the "anointing process" is working into and out of us as we continue to mature in power and authority. First, we are "set apart" (consecrated) by the Lord for His use. The initial stage of the anointing process can yield some awesome victories like David's killing of three adversaries (a lion, bear, and Goliath) after the presence of God had been "poured out" on him. Second, the act of having the anointing oil smeared on us is what can produce a greater life of worship, prayer, and obedience to the Lord as our hearts are changed by the Holy Spirit. Finally, David was anointed king over all Israel, which points to the fact that the anointing can't truly operate at its height in us until we allow the Lord to conquer us (usually after he has wrestled with the hurts, pains, sins, and embarrassing situations from our past). The pressure we at times are experiencing is the direct result of the Lord's anointing oil being worked into our lives from the external (pouring upon) to the deep inner working (rubbing in) of God's hand. This process is extremely beneficial if properly understood and embraced by those who are truly seeking to operate under His anointing.

It has been said that "David was an Old Testament king that did a New Testament thing." He was definitely the prototypical model of what a New Testament believer should become. Our next chart will help to illustrate this point:

David	NT Believer
1. Conquered a lion, bear, and Goliath	We are more than conquerors (Romans 8:37)
2. A man of praise and worship	"Speaking to yourselves in psalms, hymns and spiritual songs" (Ephesians 5:19)
3. Priest/king	"Royal Priesthood" (1 Peter 2:9, Revelation 1:6, 5:10)
4. Warrior	"Taking the sword of the Spirit" (Ephesians 6:10–20)
5. Of the seed of Abraham	The Church are of the seed of Abraham, Jesus Christ (Galatians 3:29)
6. Was rejected of men	Persecuted for the Faith (Matthew 5:11, 44, 10:23, 23:34, Romans 12:14)
7. Made a tabernacle for God's presence	We are made a spiritual house (tabernacle) for God (1 Peter 2:25, 2 Corinthians 5:1–4)

(Note: The tabernacle that David constructed is believed to be connected to the Christian Church as mentioned in Acts 15:13–18 by the apostle James in his debate with the Council at Jerusalem. This makes for an interesting study for the serious student of Bible truth).

The three anointings that David received over the course of his life and what it represented was a process for his growth and maturity. It was a type of what the Holy Spirit (the anointing) was to accomplish for the Church. The Holy Spirit was given on the day of Pentecost to the Church as an "anointing" that would assist believers in their gospel mission, as well as personal growth toward maturity (Acts 1:8).

David's Anointings	The Church's Anointings
Prophet (1 Samuel 16:1, 12–13) Proclaimer of Truth	Acts 8:4, 12, 11:20, 15:35, 20:25, 28:31; 1 Corinthians 1:18–21, 1 Corinthians 2:4, Titus 1:3
King (2 Samuel 2:4) Rules and Reigns	1 Peter 2:5, Revelation 1:6, 5:10
Priest (2 Samuel 5:1–3) Reconciles between God and men	2 Corinthians 5:18–19, Hebrew 2:17

The Church's anointing on the Day of Pentecost was its enablement to minister on behalf of God to a lost and dying world. The scriptures above help to shed light on this misunderstood truth that has been hidden from most of the twenty-first-century church in America. Acts 2:1–4 (along with Joel 2:28–29) records how God poured out His spirit (the anointing) on the Church in order to minister under the authority and power of Christ. The Church, in fact, became "Christians" (Acts 11:26) or "little anointed ones" and were expected to duplicate His ministry of preaching the gospel of the kingdom (Matthew 24:14). Casting out devils, healing the sick, raising the dead, and cleansing the lepers (Matthew 10:8, Mark 16:15–18, Luke 10:1, 17–19, Acts 3:1–10, 8:5–8, 19:1–8, 11–12). Although the Church received power and authority to do all the works mentioned above, it actually received something much more powerful, the anointing of prophet, king, and priest, as did many of God's selected Old Testament servants. The Holy Spirit given in Acts 2:1–3 is that threefold anointing experienced by those who occupied the three previous offices mentioned. What this means for the Church is that every believer who has received the anointing of the Holy Spirit has been empowered to replicate and reproduce the works of these Old Testament offices, which find their fulfillment in Jesus Christ, "the Anointed One." The three anointed offices of the

Old Testament are completed/fulfilled in the church as illustrated below:

Title	Jesus	The Church
Prophet (Proclaims Truth)	Isaiah 61:1, Luke 4:24, 24:19 Matthew 11:5, Mark 6:4	Matthew 24:14, Mark 6:12, 15
King (Rules and Reigns)	Matthew 2:2, John 10:33–38, Matthew 27:11, 29, 37, Mark 15:2, Matthew 28:18	Luke 10:117–19, Acts 1:8, Mark 16:17–20, 1 Thessalonians 1:5, 1 Peter 2:9, Revelations 1:6, 5:10
Priest (Reconciles between God and man)	Hebrew 2:17, 3:1, 4:14–15, Hebrew 5:5–10, 7	1 Peter 2:5, 9, Revelation 1:6, 5:10, 1 Corinthians 5:18–19

Jesus was a prophet, who ruled the heavens and earth as a king and functioned as a priest by His work as a mediator and reconciler for God and man. When He was baptized in the Holy Spirit in Matthew, He was literally anointed for service to operate in all three offices. Before His anointing, we never see Jesus ministering to anyone prior to His Father empowering Him. Therefore, we must conclude that the anointing was the "difference maker" in His ministry, and it should be in ours. The chart shows how the Church was anointed to be a prophetic people through the proclamation of the gospel, a kingly people who will rule and reign over this world's systems and a priestly people who are called to reconcile fallen humanity. All of these are a direct result of the anointing of the Holy Spirit being poured out at Pentecost. The book of Acts is an historical account of the ministry of the Church under the anointing of God and should be studied extensively by the Bible student to accurately identify this threefold anointing throughout the book.[38]

---

[38] Kevin J. Conner. 1989. *The Tabernacle of David.* City Christian Publishing: Portland, Oregon.

Anointed To Do Good!

———— ✑ ————

(Acts 10:38)

We have already defined the anointing as "*the anointing is the consecrating [setting apart] of a vessel [any object or person] through the empowerment of the Holy Spirit for God's specific use or purpose*" (Keith Attles).

In addition to this fundamental definition, we must include other less technical definitions like the anointing is:

- "a supernatural endowment given from the Holy Spirit,"
- "the burden removing, yoke destroying power of God,"
- "the Holy Spirit's ability delegated to the believer,"
- "the ability of God on loan to man," and
- "the grace of God in action."

All of the mentioned definitions note two main points that (1) it is *God's...*, and (2) it is His ability given to believers to set people free. Both of these themes can be seen overtly in all the definitions concerning the anointing and how the presence of the Lord's Spirit is available to set others free. Isaiah 10:27 and Isaiah 61:1–3 are outstanding scriptures which can be used to support both themes previously discussed, but Acts 10:38 brings the most clarity on what the anointing is used for and who and where does it come from.

(1) *How God* (2) *anointed* (3) *Jesus of Nazareth* (4) *with the Holy Ghost* and (5) *with power*, who (6) *went about* (7) *doing good* and (8)

70

healing all that were (9) *oppressed of the devil* for (10) *God was with Him.*

Acts 10:38 serves as a perfect model for anyone seeking to understand more about the anointing's purpose in a believer's life. There are ten keys embedded within this verse, which have the potential of creating more zeal and confidence for those seeking to minister the power of the Spirit to people in need. This text reveals ten different components that Peter used concerning how God anointed Jesus while preaching at Cornelius's house in Caesarea. The ten components are:

1. *"How God"*—Peter teaches that the anointing finds its origin from God, who is the giver of blessings and good things to His people.
2. *"Anointed"*—the Greek word used is (*chriō*), which means to smear or rub with oil, i.e. to consecrate to an office or religious service).
3. *"Jesus of Nazareth"*—the humanity of Jesus is emphasized here, indicating that He was a man who was "smeared or rubbed" for divine religious service. Without this anointing, He could not be expected to produce the results, which He enjoyed throughout His three-year-ministry experience.
4. *"With the Holy Ghost"*—the anointing agent is identified here by Peter. When Jesus received the Holy Spirit (Matthew 3:16), He received the anointing for service, which also produced tremendous power for the people bound by the kingdom of darkness.
5. *"With power"*—one of the greatest fruits of having been anointed by the Holy Spirit is that of supernatural power. The Greek word is (*dunamis*), which means "miraculous power, strength, violence, mighty (wonderful) work." From this word, we get our English word *dynamite*, which references the explosive dynamic power of the Holy Spirit.
6. *"Went about"*—one of the main purposes for the anointing is to carry it into situations that required the "yoke destroying" (Isaiah 10:27) power of God in order to bring forth

freedom. The believer is expected to go everywhere locally and globally to dispense the liberating power of the Holy Spirit. It was not given to be hoarded but to be freely given to all who came seeking its delivering power. Therefore, scriptures like Matthew 28:19–20, Mark 16:15–20, Acts 1:8, and Acts 10:38 highlight our Lord's desire to have believers "to go about" releasing the anointing of the Holy Spirit. Anointed, "Spirit-driven" evangelism will always produce works that demand divine assistance in order to accomplish the ministry task at hand. The Spirit's anointing will compel us to reach out to people in need and provide the power to meet that need.

7. *"Doing good"*—the anointing of the Holy Spirit empowers us to do "good" works on behalf of the kingdom of God. He never anoints us to condemn others, destroy churches, expose someone else's flaws publicly, or to leave people worse than before they came to us for help. The Greek word for "good" is (*euergeteō*), which means "to be philanthropic." This compound Greek word *philein*, to love, and *anthrōpos*, man, essentially means a person who "loves mankind." A philanthropic person is said to be a philanthropist or one who engages in philanthropy, which is best defined as "a desire to help mankind, especially as shown by endowments, to institutions, etc." The believer is called to bestow upon others the endowment of the Holy Spirit, which is the anointing to set people free from bondages. We are called to do "good works" as noted in Philippians 1:6, Colossians 1:10, 2 Thessalonians 1:11–12, 1 Timothy 3:1, 2 Timothy 2:21, Titus 3:1–8, and Hebrew 13:20–21, both testaments support this truth as evidenced by many servants of God that did *"good works"* under the anointing.

- Adam ruled the Garden of Eden and gave name to all of the creatures of the earth (Genesis 1:26–27, 2:19–20)

- Moses brought the Hebrews out of Egypt with a "mighty hand" (Exodus 12:1–42).
- David played anointed music for King Saul, slew the giant Goliath, and reigned as king over Israel (1 Samuel 16).
- Esther saved the Jewish people from slaughter.
- Joseph preserved the children of Israel from famine and destruction.
- Jesus set captives free and provided salvation to all.
- Peter became a major pillar in the Church.
- Stephen preached a powerful sermon under the anointing of the Holy Spirit and was stoned and received by Christ into heaven with a standing ovation (Acts 6:8, 7:1–60).
- Paul, an anointed scholar, preacher, and apostle of the early church.
- The Church, the redeemed "called out" assembly of believers who have received the "unction" (1 John 2:20) for service.

8. *"And healing all"*—the Greek word for healing is (*iáomai*), which means "to heal, cure, restore to bodily health; to heal spiritually, to make whole." The Holy Spirit's purpose is essentially to make things whole which have been bruised by the enemy (Satan). The anointing provides the healing agency of the Holy Spirit through acts of power (signs, wonders, and healings miracles) designed to free the oppressed. Divine healing has always been a provision of God's covenant with His people as seen in the Old Testament (Exodus 15:26, Deuteronomy 7:9–15, Leviticus 14:1–57, Numbers 21:4–9, Psalm 105:37, Psalm 6:2, Exodus 23:25, Psalm 103: 1–5, Matthew 4:23–24, Matthew 8:5–17, 1 Peter 2:24, 1 John 1:2, Revelation 21:4), as well as the New.

9. *"Oppressed of the devil"*—it is very important that people in general understand that it is the devil that seeks to oppress them in life (John 10:10). The Lord has given believers the

use of the Holy Spirit in order to destroy the oppressive yoke (Isaiah 10:5–6) of the enemy (Satan) and to see people restored in life. The anointing's purpose is to counter the effects of Satan by using the power of God.

10. *"For God was with him"*—believers must begin to believe the biblical record of the scriptures and see how God always made it absolutely clear who He was with by the witness and testimony of His presence (by the anointing of the Holy Spirit). Such individuals are Joseph, Moses, Samson, Elijah, David, Jesus, Paul, and many others throughout scripture. "For God was with him" is a direct reference to Jesus the Messiah (the Anointed One). The anointing is a powerful way of determining if God is truly with us.

The Holy Anointing Oil

(Exodus 30:22–23)

1 Hin = 128 ounces or six quarts

[Spices]	Myrrh +	Sweet Cinnamon +	Sweet Calamus +	Cassia +	1 Hin of Oil (6 Quarts)
[Measurements]	500 Shekels (or 200 ounces)	250 Shekels	250 Shekels	500 Shekels	3 × 500 = 1,500 Shekels

Ingredients of the Holy Anointing Oil

Myrrh
"Commiphora Myrrha" or "Balsamodendron Myrrha"

Origin: grown in Somaliland, Ethiopia, and Arabia	Grown in a faraway place, heaven
The trunk and branches exude a gum, which produces a wonderful fragrance.	Christ is the vine (trunk), and we are the branches (John 15:4–5).
Myrrh (Hebrew) means to "drop on" from a container above.	The Holy Spirit is that anointing, which runs down from heaven upon His servants (Psalm 133:2).

It was a small tree often called "thorny shrubs," and it bore a plumlike fruit.	Christ the Anointed One was considered "thorny" to the Scribes and Pharisees, but He bore anointed fruit that the multitudes ate of and were glad.
It was used as an embalming agent, medicine, perfume ointment, and incense.	The anointing's multiple uses (Acts 10:38, Isaiah 61:1–3)
It was sweet to the smell but bitter to the taste.	The anointing is usually received after enduring bitter experiences, but once obtained, produces sweet experiences.
Medically, it was used to take out soreness.	The anointing can take out the sore experiences of life (Psalm 23:5).
The sap oozes out oily, and then *solidifies* as it comes in contact with wood or stone.	The anointing of God has been given to believers so that it might "ooze" out from us "oily," but when it comes in contact with hard (stone and wood) cases it transforms to meet the need.
Myrrh oil was sometimes used in cosmetics (Esther 2:12).	The anointing beautifies our disappointments (Isa. 61:3 "to give beauty for ashes…")
It was one of the gifts the wise men presented at Jesus's birth, and it was also present at His death (Matthew 26:6–13).	This signified the awful death Christ would suffer (Isaiah 53:4–5).
Therapeutic uses: anti-inflammatory, antiseptic, antifungal, expectorant, perfume fixative, skin rejuvenator, sedative, and wound healing analgesic.	The Holy Spirit was given to also promote the character of Christ in all believers (see Galatians 5:22–23).
When mixed with wine and drunk, it produced insensibility to pain. Wine has always been understood to produce joy or an "insensibility to pain" (Isaiah 24:11, 61:3, John 2:1–11)	When the spirit of God is literally consumed by us.

Sweet Cinnamon
(Cinnamomum Zeylanicum)

The root meaning of the word *cinnamon* means "erect" or to stand upright."	The anointing will cause us to stand upright in the face of sin and ungodliness.
It grows about thirty feet high and yields small white flowers on its branches, which smell offensive, but the bark is sweet.	The anointing grows best in places of elevation and produces the purity of holiness (white flowers) in the life of its branches (see John 15:5), thus making us sweet once our offenses have been healed.
The oil is produced after the bark has been softened by *soaking* it in seawater or by *boiling* it first.	Our hard interior/exterior is softened by our soaking in the presence of the Holy Spirit or by being subjected to fiery trials (1 Peter 4:12–13).
It was commonly used in perfumes in order to enhance the fragrance.	The Holy Spirit's anointing will make us sweeter and more fragrant as we embrace the fruit of the Spirit (Galatians 5:22–23).
Its therapeutic uses were as an antibacterial, antifungal digestive, and stimulant properties.	The anointing destroys every yoke (Isaiah 10:27).
It grows only in India.	The anointing only grows as a result of the heavenly distant Holy Spirit dwelling within us.
From the fruit and coarser pieces of bark when boiled yielded fragrant oil.	When heat and pressure are applied to our lives, we release the goodness of the Lord within us.
www.victorie-inc.us/biblical_ essential_oils. html	

Sweet Calamus

(Hebrew, "Qanĕth," shaft, tube, stem, cane, bone, branch, reed, and calamus, this includes woody stems such as Arundo Donax, the Persian reed, Saccharum Agypticaum, the Arabic ghazzar).

It is a scented cane said to be found amongst the *lilies of the field.*	Lilies are white, representing purity. The sweetness of the anointing is only found in an environment of righteousness and holiness.
The reed is very *fragrant when bruised*; this includes the petals.	Broken and bruised vessels will only yield a sweet fragrance (see Mark 14: 3–8).
The oil from the reed was released by *boiling* since it is an aromatic reed.	When we are subject to situations which make us "boil," then we have a choice to release sweetness instead of bitterness.
Its knotted stalk is cut and dried and reduced to powder and then forms an ingredient in some of the most precious perfumes.	In the same way are our lives knotted and then reduced to powder through God's dealings (trials).
It was usually grown to a height of six cubits (or nine feet).	Symbolic of the nine gifts of the Spirit and nine fruit of the Spirit is maturity.
Country of origin was Nepal.	The anointing of the Holy Spirit is also from a distant place, heaven.

Cassia

(Hebrew, "guiddah" is "to split, to scrape off, to purge"), cinnamon cassia.

It has a *sweet, spicy-hot fragrance.*	The anointing of the Holy Spirit comes to make us sweeter (Galatians 5: 22–23) and fiery (Matthew 3:11)

It can be found in far-off places like China, India, and Vietnam.	The anointing's origin is heaven, a far and distant place.
Steam distillation is the best method for extracting the oil from the leaves, twigs of stalk.	Trials and tribulations are methods God uses to release the anointing oil of the Holy Spirit within us.
It gets the blood and mind in motion and is known to act as an aphrodisiac, as well as an antidepressant.	The anointing is necessary for reproduction of souls and for lasting inner peace and joy.
Its fragrance reduces drowsiness, irritability, pain, and frequency of headaches. It can relax tight muscles, cramps, joint pain, and increase blood circulation.	Isaiah 61:1–3, Isaiah 10:27, and Acts 10:38 reveal how the anointing can provide deliverance from these and many other problems we face.
This oil is very good at being a powerful germicide.	The anointing destroys every yoke of bondage, thus making it the ultimate germicide (Isaiah 10:27, Acts 10:38).
www.essential7.com/essentialoils/cassial.html	

Olive Oil

The holy anointing oil mentioned in Exodus 30:23–25 was made from the oil that was extracted from crushed olives, which was widely accepted as the best oil to be used for many products. These uses included oil for illumination, food, unguents, medicines, and sacred purposes. Therefore, the first stage in acquiring the olives involved picking them by hand in order not to spoil them usually in the fall (September to November). After picking, the olive was separated from the pulp and from a bitter watery liquid, which the ancients called "*amurca*." It was essential to avoid crushing the kernel, and this was done by partially crushing the olive, removing the kernel and the liquid and then pressing out the oil. It was usually done immediately after picking, although the olives were sometimes stored for a time on the floor of the press house. Usually one of three methods was employed to gather the oil:

1. Olives were trodden by foot (Micah 6:15).
2. Or by pounding with a pestle.
3. Or by pressing a heavy stone within a shallow stone cavity.

Sometimes in order to extract the last drops of oil from the olive (remaining pulp), it was soaked in hot water and then subjected to a second pressing in a beam or screw press. This second pressing could be carried out in stages, increasing the pressure each time. Each additional pressing produced more oil but of a lower quality. Usually three grades of olive oil were extracted. Finally, the extracted oil was allowed to stand in a rock-hewn vat or in a jar while the impurities settled.

Anointing with Oil
(Especially Olive Oil)

A. A. *Olive oil*
   1. It was believed to supply or maintain softness of the skin, suppleness of the joints, and strength to the body.
   2. It was used for smearing on a clean body after a bath.
   3. Sweet-scented (perfumed) oil preferred.
B. *Purposes for which the anointing oil were administered.*
   1. As a sign of joy and festivity (Ruth 3:3, Ecclesiastes 9:8, Amos 6:6, Luke 7:46)
   2. To soothe wounds (Isaiah 1:6, Mark 6:13, Luke 10:34)
   3. To securely seal (embalm) the dead (Mark 16:1, Luke 23:56)
   4. To show respect and esteem for someone (Psalm 23:5, Luke 7:38)
   5. As a symbol of religious services practiced by the Israelites (Exodus 30:26–29, Leviticus 8:10, 11)

6. As an act of consecration (or surrender)
7. To accompany the setting up of a memorial (Genesis 28:18, 35:14)
8. To indicate sovereign appointment, to kingship, priestly offices, or prophetic ministry (1 Samuel 16:13, Exodus 28:41, 30:30, 40:13, 15)
9. To indicate supernatural power (Isaiah 61:1–3, Matthew 3:16)
10. Sanctified objects were "set apart" for God's use (Exodus 30)
11. As a spiritual type:
    a) "Anointed" in Hebrew—Messiah
    b) "Anointed" in Greek—Christ

At first, this was a synonym for the king instituted by God's will. Second, it took on a wider meaning, sometimes being applied to foreign sovereigns (Isaiah 45:1). Third, it was applied to people in its entirety (Psalm 28:8, Hebrews 3:13). Fourth, it was applied to a prophet appointed to perform a mission of relief and comfort (Isaiah 61:1). Fifth, it ended by crystallizing the Israelites' hope of a deliverer (Daniel 9:25, Matthew 11:1–2).

The official title of Jesus (Matthew 16:16) was the Christ or "Anointed One."

C. *The User of the Anointing for God's People, We are:*
   1. *Anointed to honor someone*
      • Israel was anointed as honored. (Ezekiel 16:6–15)
      • David said, "Anoint my head with oil" (Psalm 23:5)
      • The woman who anointed Jesus's feet. (Luke 7:46)
   2. *Anointed to sanctify*
      • There is a "setting apart" or cleansing (Exodus 30: 1–38)

3. *Anointed to minister.*
   - Example for the priestly office (Exodus 30:31, 1 Samuel 16, and Isaiah 61: 1–3)
4. *Anointed to see*
   - *The blessing for seeing eyes (Matthew 13:16)*
   - Anointed eyes could see (Revelation 3:18) the Lord or comprehend His revelations.
5. *Anointed to know* (1 John 2:20, 27) for the Greek word *charisma*, which is unction, anointing.
6. *Anointed to do good* (Acts 10:38)
7. *Anointed to stand* (2 Corinthians 1:21, Revised Version Margin notes)
   This provides the following:
   a) Confidence of faith (Hebrews 3:14)
   b) A bestowed outlook of hope (Hebrews 3:6)
   c) Diligence of love (2 Peter 1:10)
   d) Braced sinews of listening (Colossians 2:7)
   e) An invigorated heart of consecration in grace, causing the heart to be established (Hebrews 13:9).
8. *Anointed to rule* (have authority). The Church has been given the Kingly authority to rule just like the Old Testament kings (see 2 Samuel 5:3; Isaiah 45:1; Matthew 16:18–19; 1 Peter 2:9; and Revelation 1:5–6, 5:10).
9. *Anointed to heal*
   a) Isaiah 10:27
   b) Isaiah 61:1–3; Luke 4:18
   c) Acts 10:38
   d) John 9:6
   e) Luke 10:1, 17–19
10. *Anointed to preach*
    - Isaiah 61:1
    - After Peter is filled (or anointed by the Holy Spirit he preaches boldly for Christ, Acts. 2:14–47

11. *Anointed to live victoriously for God.* "The yoke shall be destroyed because of the anointing" (Isaiah 10:27). *We receive*
   - courage instead of cowardice,
   - contentment instead of murmuring,
   - triumph instead of defeat,
   - love instead of hate,
   - prayer instead of prayerlessness,
   - progress instead of stagnation,
   - purpose instead of slothfulness,
   - cleanliness instead of defilement,
   - holiness instead of worldliness, and
   - Christ instead of self.
   - *(See 1 Samuel 17:1–54, David defeats Goliath because of the anointing.)*

The Anointing Defined

The following are a list of Greek and Hebrew words associated with *anoint*:

Anoint
   Hebrew, Māshach, to rub or smear
   Cûwk, to smear
   Grk. Aleiphō, to oil with perfume, anoint
   Egchriō, to besmear, anoint
   Murizō, to apply perfumed unguent to
Anointed
   Hebrew Balal, to mix, to cause to overflow, to mingle, to temper
   Mimshach, with outstretched wings. "This word is used in the sense of expansion or spreading out like the wings of an eagle mashach—to rub or smear with oil, mishachah, unction; gift, mashiyach, consecrated person; Messiah, *cûwk*, to smear, *Greek aleipho*, (see above).
   Epichrio, to smear over, anoint

Chrio, (see above)
Anointedst
    Hebrew, Mashach, to rub or smear with oil
Anointest
    Hebrew, Dashen, to anoint, to satisfy
Anointing
    Hebrew Mishchah, (see above)
    Shemen, olive, a form of grease, especially liquid and perfumed.
    Grk. Aleipho—(see above)
    Charisma, special endowment

Special Note: *Yitshar*, a noun for oil as used to produce light or figuratively to anoint (SC 3323, anointed oil).

Suk, "to pour out" (Deuteronomy 28,40, 2 Chronicles 28,15, Ruth 3,3, Ezekiel 16,9, Micah 6,15), also "to cause to pour out" (SC 5480, Hebrew) *cûwk*, to smear over (with oil) or to anoint.[39]

---

[39] James Strong. 1996. *The New Strong's Exhaustive Concordance of the Bible.* Nashville: Thomas Nelson Publisher.

    John F. Campbell, Donald K. Witmer, and John A. Witmer. 2000. *Theological Wordbook.* Thomas Nelson Publisher.

Reasons for the Anointing

———— ⚘ ————

The Holy Anointing Oil mentioned in Exodus 30 can be best understood to be the tangible evidence of the Holy Spirit's activity within the believer's life and ministry. Therefore, if we examine the scriptures, we should be able to find convincing evidence that the reason God gave the anointing (oil) was to provide a means of strength or (empowerment for service to His people). This can be confirmed by Isaiah 10:27, which says, "*And it shall come to pass in that day, that his burden shall be taken away from off thy shoulder, and his yoke from off thy neck, and the yoke shall be destroyed because of the anointing.*"

Here the prophet Isaiah is prophesying a message of hope to Israel because the Lord has released the Assyrian army to be an instrument of chastisement and judgment for His rebellious people. Under the leadership of Sennacherib, king of Assyria in 722 BC, they became a rod of God's anger (Isaiah 10:5–6) toward His hypocritical nation. God's prophetic imagery of "yoke" being placed on Israel's neck symbolized a heavy wooden harness used to joint two (or more) oxen together for the sake of working (plowing) a field or to do heavy manual work for the master. Isaiah's prophecy is spoken to give a hope to a remnant of righteous followers of God who would find themselves included in the pending judgment on Israel. The Lord says that this yoke which has produced hardship, which will eventually be destroyed (*châbal*, to wind tightly as a rope, i.e. to bind *specifically* by a pledge; *figure*—to pervert, destroy; also to writhe in pain) because of the *anointing*. The word in Hebrew used here for anointing is (*shemen*), a form of grease, especially liquid (as from the olive), which is usually perfumed. Figuratively, this word means "richness," which within the context of the prophecy can mean that the Lord would destroy the enemy's oppressive hand by restoring the Spirit and favor (richness) to His people once again. It is with the help of these two graces that believers can always live a life free from the oppression of the enemy (Satan) because:

a) In 2 Corinthians 3:17, it says, "Now the Lord is that Spirit: and where the Spirit of the Lord is, there is liberty" (liberty/ eleutheria, freedom, generosity, independence).

b) In Luke 1:30, it says, *"And the angel said unto her, 'Fear not, Mary: for thou hast found favor with God.'"*

(It is important to note that this favor produced the "Anointed One" who would destroy every yoke and burden plaguing humanity, vs. 31).

The burden removing yoke destroying power (grace) of God called the "anointing" is what the Lord was promising to "pour out" (a liquid perfumed oil) on Israel for their deliverance. This promise is not only good for Old Testament followers of God but for the New Testament followers of the Christ (Christos the "Anointed One").

The reasons for the anointing (an enabling empowerment of God for service) can be found throughout the Bible for a multitude of circumstances namely:

1. Consecrate (set apart) things for God's specific use (Exodus 29:29)
2. Empower His leaders for service (see Judges 3:10, 6:34, 11:29, 13:25, 1 Samuel 16:12–13, Isaiah 61:1, and Acts 10:38)
3. Break the power of the enemy (Satan) (Isaiah 10:27, Acts 10:38).
4. "Preach good tidings unto the meek" (Isaiah 61:1). "Your captivity is over!" (Matthew 4:23; John 7:19–22).
5. "Bind up the brokenhearted," to restore those of a wounded spirit (John 4:1–30).

6. "Proclaim liberty to the captives," this is the message of the "kingdom of God," that all who were enslaved to Satan can now be free in Christ.

7. "The opening of the prison to then that are bound," the Spirit of God has set you free from captivity (John 8:36).

8. "Proclaim the acceptable year of the Lord." This was a proclamation of freedom to all who were in debt or slavery; every fifty years you were set free (Leviticus 25).

9. "The day of vengeance of our God." This is God's Judgment Day on sin and rebellion toward him (Jeremiah 46:10).

10. "Comfort all that mourn" (John 11:1, 11–44). The Holy Spirit is also known as the "Comforter" in John 14:16, 26, 15:26, 16:17.

11. "Appoint unto them that mourn in Zion." Zion is an Old Testament type of the Church where many believers have yet to experience their healing and restoration.

12. "Give unto them beauty for ashes," the beauty of holiness is exchanged for the ashes of sin (1 Chronicles 16:29, 2 Chronicles 20:21, Psalm 29:2, Psalm 39:11, Psalm 50:2, 96:9).

13. "Oil of joy for mourning," the anointing of God when used to heal and do miracles can produce great joy in a city (Acts 8:4–8).

14. "The garment of praise for the spirit of heaviness," worship invites the anointing or presence of God, which in turn sets us free (1 Samuel 16:14–23).

15. "That they might be called trees of righteousness, the planting of the Lord," the presence of God helps to establish a life of stability founded in righteousness and grace.

16. "That he might be glorified." The anointing power brings glory to God and His kingdom. (John 11:1–4, 40, Luke 17:11–18)

17. "Open blinded eyes" (John 9:6). Also, 2 Corinthians 3:13–14 and 4:4, which helps us to understand that the unsaved are blinded, but the anointing can make them see.

18. Duplicate the evangelical ministry of our Lord through the ministry gifts listed in Ephesians 4:11–12.
19. To do the works of Jesus (Matthew 28:16–20, Mark 16:14–20, Acts 1:8).
20. To reproduce the Spirit of Christ in believers (John 15:7–8, 16, Galatians 5: 22–25).
21. To bear witness of a person's office and calling (1 Samuel 16:1, 1 Kings 19:16, Isaiah 61:1 with Luke 7:19–22).
22. To be taught the truths of God (John 16:13, 1 John 2:20, 27).
23. To live a holy life, the anointing of the Holy Spirit is a grace given to believers to encourage holiness (John 16:7–11, Romans 1:3–4, 6:15–23, Ephesians 4:21–25, 1 Thessalonians. 4:7, Hebrews 12:14).

Note: The Holy Spirit is the anointing of God that was given to the Church on the day of Pentecost to perfect (mature) both the fruit (Galatians 5:22–23) and gifts (I Corinthians 12:7–11) for ministry effectiveness.

Restrictions for Using the Anointing Oil

God commanded Moses to pay strict adherence to his prohibitions against casually using the holy anointing oil in Exodus 30:31–33, which says,

> And thou shalt speak unto the children of Israel, saying, this shall be an holy anointing oil unto me throughout your generations. Upon man's flesh shall it not be poured, neither shall ye make any other like it, after the composition of it: it is holy, and it shall be holy unto you. Whosoever compoundeth any like it, or whosoever putteth any of it upon a stranger, shall even be put off from his people.

The Holy Anointing Oil Restrictions

Restriction	Truth
Not to be poured out indiscriminately (carelessly), (Exodus 30:32).	A person's flesh or body was off-limits for the holy anointing oil because fleshly (carnal) things cause problems when mixed with spiritual things.
Not to be imitated (Exodus 30:32).	Israel was warned to never duplicate the ingredients of God's holy anointing oil, thus signifying that man-made schemes and devices are never a substitute for the supernatural enablement of God through the anointing of the Holy Spirit.
Never forsake the divine formula (Exodus 30:23–24, 35:10–19).	God told Moses repeatedly throughout the building of the tabernacle to build it according to the pattern (blueprint), (Exodus 25:9, 40, Numbers 8:4). Obedience to God's design minimizes the works of the flesh!
It was for use in the Holy Place (Exodus 31:11).	The Holy Place was where the Golden Candlestick, Table of Shewbread, and the Altar of Incense abode in Moses's Tabernacle. The anointing of God upon believers works best when we commune with each other in unity (Psalm 133) at the Table of Shewbread or when we allow the anointing oil to burn deep within our hearts producing the light of Christ like the Golden Candlestick. Also, like the Altar of Incense, we function best when there is a combination of prayer and worship emanating from our lives to God's throne (see Revelation 5:8–9, 8:4).
It was never to be used without leadership's oversight and inspection (Exodus 39:32–43).	The anointing of the Holy Spirit works best when God's people are submitted to church leadership. There is accountability, inspection of our lifestyle, and the oversight of seasoned ministry to assist us in the development of our

	giftings. Leviticus 21:12 gives a final restriction to all who would minister to the Lord in the holy place (Sanctuary—"neither shall He go out of the sanctuary of His God; for the crown of the anointing oil of His God is upon Him: I am the Lord." The High Priest as the senior official of the tabernacle was given a stern warning not to leave the sanctuary where He was responsible to minister to God on behalf of the people. Anointed people and especially leaders must not forget that they have been anointed to direct their ministry to the Lord first by ministering to Him with our prayers and songs of worship. We are never to leave the "holy place" (or in other words the place of holiness) to pursue other tasks and events over that of seeking Him.
It was not to be poured upon strangers.	The "stranger" to an Israelite was anyone who wasn't born within their family tradition, but through Christ, NT believers are no longer strangers (Ephesians 2:11–22, Galatians 3:28, Colossians 3:10–11).
Disobedience to these restrictions would mean being "cut off" from the covenant community (Israel).	Disobedience to Christ's commandments concerning kingdom living will result in out being "cut off" from the anointing of the Holy Spirit (Luke 9:62, Ephesians 4:30).

Anointing the Unsanctified

———— ⌘ ————

Upon man's flesh shall it not be poured, neither shall
ye make and other like it, after the composition of
it: it is holy, and it shall be holy unto you.

—Exodus 30:32

Within this scripture is where the heart of God revealed for producing the holy anointing oil. It was intended to be an exclusive part of the priestly office that of anointing *Aaron and his sons* and all the vessels for Tabernacle ministry, including the structure and furniture. Everything anointed with the oil was expected to be "holy," both people and all materials being used. The Lord gave three specific instructions pertaining to the anointing:

- Never pour it on a man's flesh.
- Make nothing like it.
- It was to be regarded as holy.

We must understand all three stipulations if we are going to be able to appreciate the Lord's reasoning and request for these prohibitions. First, the Lord warns about putting the holy anointing oil upon a person's flesh. The word *flesh* in this verse is *basar* (flesh), and it means "body, skin, nakedness, self [man or animal], and is commonly used to refer to the 'principal constituent of the body, human, or animal.'" What we can gather from these definitions is that the Lord prohibited the contact between the sacred oil and human flesh

91

(carnality). The oil of heavenly origin (as requested by God) was never to be brought into contact with earthly flesh, except as ordered by God Himself (David) because the two are opposed to each other. Greater insight into the word *flesh* must be sought from its New Testament usage. The word *flesh* in Greek is *sarx*, and it means "the meat of an animal—by implication, *human nature*. The truth of what the flesh represented in the Old Testament has now been uncovered in the New because in God's mind, the flesh always represented '*human nature.*'" The holy anointing oil was never to be mixed with the ways of human nature because the result would usually end-up disastrous for everyone involved. King Saul was an excellent example of a person who was anointed with this oil and yet exhibited "fleshly" living throughout his entire reign as king. Another individual who deserves some attention regarding this matter is Samson (Judges 14–16). Here is a man who was "anointed or empowered" by the Holy Spirit to act as a deliverer on behalf of God's people over their enemies. The presence of God on Samson's life was, without doubt, quite remarkable, but his fleshly desires eventually ruined his anointing, life, and ministry service to the Lord as seen in the chart below:

The Anointing's Empowerment	Works of the Flesh
1. Dedicated to the Lord	Loved strange women.
2. Exceedingly strong	Broke his vow by allowing his head to be shaved.
3. Great warrior	Had his eyes put out.
4. Man of faith	Was imprisoned by his enemy.
5. Killed a lion	The Spirit of the Lord left him.
6. Killed thirty Philistines	Was mocked and ridiculed.
7. Killed one thousand soldiers	Was adulterous.
8. Very wise	Allowed his purpose to be shortened by his fleshly living.

9.	His final act of heroism ended up causing him to kill more people in one day than his entire life and ministry as a deliverer/judge.	Eventually lost what made him great, the anointing of the Holy Spirit.

Samson's lack of discipline over his fleshly (carnal) desires is what destroyed him in the end, and likewise, we ought to learn from his and other examples in scripture of how not to live if we want to be anointed vessels for the Lord.

In the New Testament, the Apostle Paul constantly warned against allowing the flesh (human nature and desires) to rule us. In Romans 7:14–24, Paul records his personal struggle with the temptations of the flesh, which may be the direct result of not having a renewed mind that is produced by the Holy Spirit and the word of God in a particular area of one's life. When these two powers are joined together within a believer's life, then the believer can experience the power of a renewed life. Roman's 8:5–14 provides an excellent understanding for how the carnal mind (fleshly thoughts) is at war with a person submitted to the Holy Spirit (the Anointing). Verse 9 says, "*But ye are not in the flesh, but in the Spirit, if so be that the Spirit of God dwell in you. Now if any man has not the Spirit of Christ, he is none of his.*"

The emphasis of this verse is on the fact that the New Testament believer is not expected to live a life in the flesh by carnal thoughts which govern one's life but is expected to live in the Spirit (or in the presence of the anointing). Therefore, carnal or fleshly living will cause us to be literally at odds with the purposes of God revealed by the anointing, so believers must seek to subdue their evil desires, lustful passions, and carnal thoughts that have separated them from a walk in the Spirit (or anointing). The Apostle Paul also gives warning of the effects of a fleshly walk and its consequences when he addressed the church in Galatia. Galatians 5:16–21 says:

The Spirit and Flesh are in Constant Battle

This I say then, Walk in the Spirit, and ye shall not fulfill the lust of the flesh. For the flesh lusteth against the Spirit, and the Spirit against the flesh: and these are contrary the one to the other: so that ye cannot do the things that ye would. But if ye be led of the Spirit, ye are not under the law.

Results of the Flesh

Now the works of the flesh are manifest, which are these: adultery, fornication, uncleanness, lasciviousness, idolatry, witchcraft, hatred, variance, emulations, wrath, strife, seditions, heresies, envyings, murders, drunkenness, revelings, and such like of the which I tell you before as I have also told you in time past that they which do such things shall not inherit the kingdom of God.

The Works of the Flesh

- *Fornication* (*porneia*), a broad word including all forms of immoral and sexual acts. It is premarital sex and adultery; it is abnormal sex, all kinds of sexual vice.
- *Uncleanness* (*akatharsia*), moral impurity, doing things that dirty, pollute, and soil life.
- *Lasciviousness* (*aselgeia*), filthiness, indecency, shamelessness. It means unrestricted evil thoughts and behavior. It is giving in to brutish and lustful desires, a readiness for any pleasure. A lascivious person doesn't try to hide his sin but does it openly and unashamedly.
- *Idolatry* (*eidololatreia*), the worship of idols, whether mental or made by man's hands, the worship of some idea of what God is like, of an image of God within a person's mind, the giving of one's primary devotion (time and energy) to something other than God.

- *Witchcraft (pharmakeia)*, sorcery, the use of drugs or of evil spirits to gain control over the lives of others or over one's own life. It includes all forms of seeking the control of one's fate, including astrology, telling, crystals, and other forms of witchcraft.
- *Hatred (echthrai)*, enmity, hostility, animosity. It is hatred that lingers and is held for a long, long time, a hatred that is deep within.
- *Variance (ereis)*, strife, discord, contention, fighting, struggling, quarreling, dissension, wrangling. It means that a man fights against another person in order to get something—position, promotion, prosperity, honor, and recognition. He deceives, doing whatever has to be done to get what he is after.
- *Emulations (zeloi)*, jealousy, wanting and desiring to have what someone else has. It may be material things, recognition, honor, or position.
- *Wrath (thumoi)*, bursts of anger, indignation; a violent, explosive temper; quick-tempered explosive reactions that arise from stirred and boiling emotions.
- *Strife (eritheiai)*, conflict, struggle, fight, contention, friction, dissention; a party spirit, a cliquish spirit.
- *Seditions (dichostasiai)*, divisions, rebellion, standing against others, splitting off from others.
- *Heresies (aireseis)*, rejecting the fundamental beliefs of God, Christ, the Scriptures, and the church, believing and holding to some teaching other than the truth.
- *Envyings (phthonoi)*, this word goes beyond jealousy. It is the spirit...that wants not only the things that another person has but begrudges the fact that the person has them. It also wants not only the things to be taken away from the person but wants him to suffer through the loss of them.
- *Murders (phonoi)*, to kill, to take the life of another person.
- *Drunkenness (methai)*, taking drink or drugs to affect one's senses for lust or pleasure, becoming tipsy or intoxicated,

partaking of drugs, seeking to loosen moral restraint for bodily pleasure.

- *Revelings* (*komoi*), carousing, uncontrolled license, indulgence, and pleasure, taking part in wild parties or in drinking parties, lying around indulging in feeding the lusts of the flesh, orgies.

This warning is given to ensure that believers understand the consequences of their actions when we subject ourselves to carnal desires, which potentially can destroy or seriously alter God's plan for our lives. Paul says, "They which do such things shall not inherit the kingdom of God." Let us endeavor to live and walk in the Spirit and not allow the Lord's anointing to come in contact with our fleshly ways.

The next warning, we receive is to never "*make anything like it.*" This prohibition given by the Lord to Moses was to safeguard the divine formula from being duplicated to restrict the mixing of it to only the perfumer (apothecary) and to restrain just anyone from making and applying the holy anointing oil to anybody outside of the ordinance of God.

The anointing oil was never to be duplicated by taking the four ingredients (myrrh, sweet cinnamon, sweet calamus, cassia) and mixing them in olive oil. There are many today that have tried to duplicate the anointing of the Holy Spirit by using marketing techniques, showmanship, education, or worldly networking schemes to appear anointed by the Lord. Instead of being a people who exhibit the evidence of the Lord's anointing by preaching powerful testimonies of God's goodness, healing the sick, casting out devils, and the like today's church is content on having a "form of godliness but denies the power of God" (2 Timothy 3:5). Have we tried to "duplicate" the anointing of God with schemes and tactics, which are prevalent in our society, or have we simply become unwilling to respect the precious (cost) of his anointing for our lives? Whichever is true, believers and leadership must begin to seek the Lord for discernment so that we can distinguish the genuine from a counterfeit anointing. Character, integrity, humility, love, and self-control are just a few characteristics of what an anointed person of the Lord should exhibit in their life and ministry.

In Acts 19:11–16, we are told how Paul wrought special miracles and healed many diseased people while in Ephesus, but there were a group of men who coveted his anointing. They were the seven sons of Sceva, the sons of the chief priest of the Jewish people. These sons watched the anointing of the Holy Spirit do wonders amongst the people, and they desired it also but had not been submitted to Jesus's lordship or the anointing of the Holy Spirit. They tried to "duplicate" the works of Paul by trying to cast a devil out of a man but soon learned that they were different from Paul once the demonic spirit overcame them. In Acts 8:9–24, we read about Simon the Sorcerer who used witchcraft to exalt himself over the people of Samaria "as some great one." Philip, a man anointed with the Holy Spirit and power, eventually had an encounter with Simon. The people of Samaria from the least to the greatest believed Simon to be "the great power of God" because of his magic and sorceries demonstrated before them. Phillip passes through Samaria and evangelizes the region through the preaching of the kingdom message, baptizing many converts and through the signs and wonders, which he did. Simon eventually repents of these things and decides to join Phillip on his missionary tour throughout Samaria. After beholding the miracles Phillip wrought, Simon desires to have this power of the Spirit and offers Peter and John (who joined Simon at a later date) money so that he could duplicate these awesome works as well (vs. 18). Simon inquires how he too can have this power in verse 19, which says: "*Saying, 'Give me also this power, that on whomsoever I lay hands, he may receive the Holy Ghost.'*"

But what we see happen is a similar pronouncement of judgment in Exodus 30:33 ("shall even be *cut off* from his people"), similar to that of Acts 8:20 ("Thy money *perish* with thee, because thou hast thought that the gift of God nay be purchased with money"). Both scriptures convey the idea of extreme punishment for those who would presume to handle the anointing of God carelessly. The gift of the Lord's anointing through the Holy Spirit is a precious endowment that should never be duplicated by anyone other than our Divine Perfumer, the Lord Jesus Christ.

The art of the apothecary (perfumer) was designated by the Lord to be the only individual(s) who were licensed to compound (mix) all of these precious ingredients together for holy (consecrated) purposes as defined in Exodus 30:26–30. Every component used by the perfumer was to be included in this mixture because the Lord knew that characteristics of His nature were to be exemplified in us once we received the baptism of the Holy Spirit. As we have already noted, every spice yielded specific qualities that are to be "worked into" our lives as the result of having His spirit abide within us. The Godhead (the apothecary) ordered the giving of the Holy Spirit to the Church in order to create the characteristics of each principle spice within our lives; thus creating a "perfumed" people of love and grace to serve humanity. The Father, Son, and Holy Spirit's desire like the apothecary is to make a people who have internalized the qualities of the principal spices and who can now be "poured out" to heal the ailments of society and its people.

The final warning found in Exodus 30:32–33 was that "*just anyone*" could not compound (mix) these ingredients together with the intent to duplicate the holy anointing oil. Two things ought to be noted here: (1) only the perfumer (apothecary) could make it, and (2) it was not to be put upon a "stranger" (vs. 33). Only ordained or chosen leaders called of God were responsible for making the holy anointing oil, thus typifying the responsibility of church leadership's ordination to assist in the development of believers in their ability to minister under the anointing. Only the Godhead is able to formulate the spiritual anointing oil to be poured out and upon believers in general (Joel 2:28–29, Acts 2: 1–3). Another truth the Lord placed upon the holy anointing oil was that it was never to be poured on a "stranger." The Hebrew term is (*zūwr*), a stranger, foreigner, profane, specifically (active participle) to commit adultery. "Perhaps the root idea is that of deviating, nonacquaintance, or unrelatedness." Anyone who was not a part of God's covenant community in the sense of being a follower of Jehovah was considered to be a heathen and a "stranger from the covenants of promise" (see Ephesians 2:11–12).

Anyone who was outside the blessing of the Abrahamic covenant and who was not a follower of the Mosaic Law should not even be considered a worthy recipient of such a divine empowerment. There are many in the Church today who have not fully or in part exhibit a genuine commitment to Christ and who should not expect to receive his anointing for service (Acts 2:38). The Church must guard against people outside of its covenant community from trying to infiltrate and utilize the anointing as demonstrated in Acts 19:11–16 (the seven sons of Sceva).

The last prohibition given to Moses was to respect the holy anointing oil as being "holy." Holiness is perhaps the primary attribute of God reiterated throughout the Old Testament (Exodus 15:11, Psalm 89:35, Amos 4:2, 1 Chronicles 16:29, 2 Chronicles 20:21, Isaiah 40:25, 2 Kings 19:22, Jeremiah 50:29, Ezekiel 39:7) and was used to designate those anointed of God as being set apart for service to him. The Hebrew word used for holy in Exodus 30:32 is *gôdesh*, which means a "sacred place or thing, consecrated [thing], dedicated [thing], hallowed [thing], holiness, holy, saint, sanctuary." This was the principal word used for "*holy*" in the Old Testament about 297 times, whereas "*hagios*" was used 162 times in the New Testament. The word meant "sacred (phys. pure, mor., blameless or religious, cer., consecrated), (most) holy, saint." Concerning both Hebrew and Greek words the *Theological Wordbook* makes this comment:

> *From the use of the words "holy" and "holiness" in Scripture, as well as from the meaning of the Hebrew and Greek words (gōdeš and its derivatives in Hebrew and hagios and its derivatives in Greek), the concept signifies something or someone who is separate and set apart or consecrated.*
>
> *God alone is inherently holy, but He is also able to make His creatures holy in the sense of being morally pure.*
>
> *By choosing Israel to be His special nation, God made the Israelites holy, that is, separated from other peoples and consecrated to Him (Exodus 31:13).*

> God also makes many inanimate objects holy in the sense of setting things apart for sacred use (Exodus 29:37, 40:9–10, Leviticus2:3, 10, 6:25–27, Numbers 4:15–16, 16:37). Obviously, no moral purity resides in these things, but they are dedicated to the service of God and, therefore, are holy. Christians are occasionally spoken of as holy in the sense of being separated to God (2 Timothy 2:21, 1 Peter 2:9), but more often the emphasis is on holiness as moral purity.
>
> Because God views Christians as holy and blameless, He exhorts them to become as morally pure in their daily lives as possible by the help of the indwelling Holy Spirit. Being holy means maintaining purity of thoughts and attitudes (Hebrew 4:12, Psalm 139:23), addition to correct deeds.

The idea being conveyed in Exodus 30:32 was that only people who the Lord designated as holy were able to have the anointing oil applied to their lives. This act identified them as being holy, consecrated, or set apart for divine usage. Holiness has an important role to play in the anointing of God because the Spirit's presence will not abide where there is unconfessed sin. Purity of mind, body, and spirit are what are well pleasing to the Lord, and He will reward them who keep themselves "unspotted from the world" and its lusts (James 1:27, 1 John 2:15–17). The Church must protect the precious endowment of the Holy Spirit that has been entrusted to us by modeling our lives after Christ and by limiting any contamination from the systems of this world (2 Corinthians 6:14–18, 1 Corinthians 6:9–19, 1 Corinthians 3:17, 1 Peter 1:16). Sin and unrighteous living amongst believers is the main reason why the anointing of the Holy Spirit isn't being poured out in massive doses because we are, in fact, grieving His spirit (Ephesians 4:30). Therefore, we must better monitor how we live, relate to others, and serve the Lord as a people called to be sanctified and holy as a New Testament priesthood (1 Peter 2:5, 9,

Revelation 1:6, 5:10), which has been anointed with holy oil in the likeness of the Old Testament priesthood.

Believers are to walk in a manner that glorifies Christ and acknowledge the cross' impact on our ability to live the crucified life (Luke 9:23, Romans 6:6, Galatians 2:20, 6:14, Colossians 3:30). Death to our selfish ways can be very difficult and challenging, but if accomplished, it can produce an anointed-filled life of strength and blessing to others. The Apostle Paul reminds us of our responsibility to walk the Christian life (Ephesians 4:17–32) and to be imitators of God (Ephesians 5:1–21). If we heed his advice in these chapters, we can expect to be recipients of the Lord's New Testament anointing from the Holy Spirit (Acts 2:1–3).

The Costly Anointing

I have often wondered what it would take to be truly anointed of
the Lord? After many years of studying various truths and principles found in God's word, I believe I have discovered some marvelous
components of this multifaceted question. Let me begin by review-
ing a powerful statement given by Christ in Luke 14:26–30 when
He said:

> *If any man come to me,*
> *And hate not his father and mother*
> *And wife and children and brethren*
> *And sisters yea, and his own life also,*
> *He cannot be my disciple.*
> *And whosoever doth not*
> *Bear his cross and come*
> *After me, cannot be my disciple.*
> *For which of you*
> *Intending to build a tower,*
> *Sitteth not down first and*
> *Counteth the cost, whether he have*
> *Sufficient to finish it?*

In this passage of scripture, Jesus reveals a principle truth of
what it takes to live, serve, and advance in the kingdom of God. Jesus
says that if we cannot deny our allegiance to others closest to us and
embrace self-denial, we cannot be His disciple. Next He tells us our
willingness to "bear His cross" (our personal ability to bear suffering

and shame associated with His death) is essential; otherwise, we cannot be is disciple. Jesus established these truths within the minds of His hearers in order to lead them to a point where they must decide for themselves if they are able, willing, and ready for such a life commitment to Him. He says:

> *For which of you*
> *Intending to build a tower,*
> *Sitteth not down first and*
> *Counteth the cost, whether he have*
> *Sufficient to finish it?*

Jesus encourages those who choose to follow Him to take a serious look at their lives and what they may have to lose to follow Him. First, "count the cost" or sit down and "enumerate the expense" (calculate the cost). The wisdom Jesus gives us is to estimate the amount of time, energy, and sacrifice it will take to serve Him before embarking on this journey. Later in Luke 14:29–33, this recommendation is strongly reinforced by the example of making war with an invading king and counting the cost to see if, in fact, you can win the battle before it even started. A life in service to Jesus is one of self-sacrifice, self-denial, and the surrendering of our will to the will of the Master, the Lord Jesus Christ.

Jesus is able to ask this of us because the Father asked this of Him as recorded in Paul's letter to the believers at Philippi in Philippians 2:5–11.

> *Let this mind be in you, which was also in*
> *Christ Jesus: who being in the form of God thought*
> *it not robbery to be equal with God: but made him-*
> *self of no reputation and took upon Him the form*
> *of a servant and was made in the likeness of men:*
> *and being found in fashion as a man, He humbled*
> *himself, and became obedient unto death, even the*
> *death of the cross. Wherefore God also hath highly*
> *exalted him, and given him a name, which is above*

every name: that at the name of Jesus, every knee should bow of things in heaven and things in earth, and things under the earth, and that every tongue should confess that Jesus Christ is Lord, to the glory of God the Father.

This mindset Paul is asking of the followers of Christ is one of selflessness, which was exemplified throughout Jesus's life and ministry while on earth. His high level of selflessness and obedience to the will of His Father is what allowed Him to be exalted by being given the "name above every name." Christ's ability to "count the cost" for the price of man's redemption is what enabled Him to die the death of the cross for our salvation. In fact, the word *redemption* implies that a price or cost had to be paid for man's total redemption from sin. As we follow Jesus's example to willingly lay down our lives for a cause, we will always be confronted with having to choose whether or not to deny ourselves the pleasures this life can afford or to "count the cost" and "pay the price" for what we perceive to be the will of God for our lives. This is the example we are left to mimic as we strive to become Christ's disciples (an adherent, a disciplined one, an obedient follower of their teacher).

The calling to this level of discipleship was evident in both the Old and New Testaments as characterized by:

OLD TESTAMENT

*Abraham following the Lord
Job following the Lord,
David following Saul,
Elisha following Elijah*

NEW TESTAMENT

*Jesus and the twelve disciples,
Barnabas and Paul,
Paul and Timothy*

All of the examples listed above can be used to confirm the idea that disciples (or mentoree) are asked to give up their purposes and to conform to the will of their teacher/mentor. If they were able to do this successfully, they had to "count the cost" of their discipleship and willingly follow their teacher/mentor.

Church history bears witness to the ideology and methodology of preparing willing disciples to forsake their families, appetites, lusts for the world system, sexual pleasure, and a host of other things in order to serve a person or a cause. They had to "count the cost" for spirituality empowerment or a greater revelation of the divine. This can be clearly seen in what was called the "Monastic movement," which was a time when believers and church leaders felt it necessary to be set apart from the world's influence in order to live a more holy and disciplined life before the Lord. As the concern for moral purity grew, the church found itself drifting into greater levels of self-denial practices, which led to martyrdom, Encratism, and eventually monasticism. Followers of the encratic movement would often display extreme practices to show their level of commitment to the Lord. One of their practices led some believers (Encratites) to perform self-castration celebrated by running through the streets, holding one's testicles aloft. As this movement continued to grow, it eventually led to the practice of "anchoritism," which in Greek means "to withdraw." One of the greatest contributors to this movement and regarded as one of the most influential church leaders ever was Saint Augustine (AD 354–430), the bishop of Hippo and doctor of the Latin Church.

Saint Augustine formed a religious community in North Africa where he lived for thirty-four years in a monastic community. It was there that he struggled with the "inner self" as he sought to understand the mind, will, and body and their effect on a believer's relationship with God and Christ. His thoughts and reflections on this topic were written in his autobiographical work entitled, *Confessions*. As the church continued to move forward, the Middle Ages produced people like Gregory the Great, Maximus the Confessor, Bernard of Clairvaux, St. Frances of Assisi, and St. Thomas Aquinas, who tried to enhance the believer's walk with God by adding to or subtracting from the practice of asceticism. Here are just a few examples of how mankind tried to bridge the gap between himself and the Lord. Church history is full of similar accounts of people willing to forsake everything in order to "be" Christ's disciple. Their religious fervor should not be overlooked because of unconventional practices and methodologies used throughout Christendom. The fact remains that self-denial, self-sacrifice, or any other extreme form of discipleship has always been accepted as a means for drawing closer to God. Our present "Westernized" theology often rejects such levels of dedication to the Lord as foolishness, extremism, or "works-based," but this can't be supported by the Old or New Testament biblical history. If we want more of God, we must be willing to "pay the price" by dying to selfishness and works of the flesh Galatians 5:22. The anointing will cost us something!

Another interesting fact associated with the anointing oil mentioned in Exodus 30:22–23 are its ingredients. All of the principal spices find their place of origin in a foreign land, which took great expense to import these products to the Promise Land. The following chart will help illustrate this point:

Spice	*Place of Origin*
Myrrh	Somaliland, Ethiopia, and Arabia
Sweet Cinnamon	France
Cassia	Vietnam, India, Southeast China
Sweet Calamus	India

The chart above can somehow validate the idea of the "cost of the anointing." It seems that anything worthwhile comes at some expense in order to separate those who simply want it from those who will willingly pay the price for it. Here is a list of people who were willing to pay the price for the anointing (or the right to be used by the Holy Spirit):

Abraham left his homeland and had to willingly sacrifice his son, Isaac.

Joseph hated by his brothers, was falsely accused, and sent to prison for thirteen years.

Moses left his powerful position in Egypt and wandered forty years in the wilderness.

David left his father's house, fought Goliath, and fled from Saul for seven years.

Elisha served Elijah in order to receive a double portion of the anointing.

Jeremiah was thrown in prison because of his prophetic preaching concerning the fall of Jerusalem by the Babylonians.

Paul, as recorded in 2 Corinthians 11:16–33 and 2 Corinthians 12:1–10, his trials were part of his "paying the price" for such a high level of usage by the Lord.

Stephen paid the ultimate price of his life for the preaching of the gospel (Acts 7:54–60, Martyrdom).

Peter was eventually crucified upside down according to church history.

Many others like Dietrich Bonhoffer, Watchmen Nee, John Wycliffe, Martin Luther, John Carey, Mother Teresa, and many others gave up their all in service to the Lord. In addition to God's grace to assist us in ministry, like all of the individuals listed above, we must constantly "count the cost" and "pay the price" to be partakers of His glory.

Unlike the people above, today's church in America doesn't believe we must embrace a life of self-sacrifice or even persecution for righteousness sake (Matthew 5:10). Instead, we try to invoke God's grace over every situation without taking into account our role or responsibility in a matter. The equation for obtaining this costly anointing should look like this:

God's Grace +	Self-Sacrifice	= The Holy Spirit's Anointing
(His Divine Strength)	(Dying to Self)	(Power)

The question we must ask ourselves is, "What must I do as a believer to 'pay the price' for this costly anointing?" Here are a few suggestions:

1. *Intercessory prayer* (Numbers 16:46–50)

Prayer is simply a means for communicating with God and intercessory prayer involves petitioning God on another's behalf. Therefore, prayer becomes an act of self-denial, which seeks to benefit others because of a motivation to see another person set free from any form of bondage. It has always been regarded as the pinnacle act of selflessness, devotion, and love for another.

2. *Fasting* (Daniel 10:1–21)

Fasting is abstaining from food, drink, or a specified pleasure for a period of time to enhance spiritual sensitivity, power, or authority over the flesh. This form of self-denial has historically been proven to turn impossible situations around in a miraculous way because fasting helps us to receive of God's grace. The Lord's help and assistance has been seen throughout the Bible in both testaments (Exodus 34:28, 1 Samuel 1:7–8, 2 Samuel 12:16–23, Nehemiah 1:4, Daniel 1:12–16, Daniel 6:18, Matthew 4:2, Acts 13:2–3).

3. *Holiness* (Romans 12:1)

Holiness is a general term to indicate sanctification, separation from sin or anything impure as compared to God or His holy word. This is perhaps the greatest attribute of God that He desires to become a part of those who serve and follow Him. One of the most challenging tasks God asks of us is to live and maintain a life of moral wholeness through holiness. In return for such a level of self-sacrifice, He rewards us by His being faithful to fulfill all covenantal promises and blessings for our lives. He also allows a greater measure of His anointing and power to flow through us in order to meet the needs of humanity. The pursuit of holiness is and will be of tremendous benefit for the Christian pursuing more of God (Exodus 39:30, Leviticus 10:8, Leviticus 11:44, Psalm 37:27, Isaiah 52:1, Zechariahs 8:3, 2 Corinthians 16:14–17, 2 Corinthians 7:1, 2 Timothy 2:19–22).

4. *Humility* (Philippians 2:5–11)

One of the greatest attributes a believer can possess is that of humility. This can be defined as a lowliness of mind in regard to self, which manifests itself in gentleness of spirit. This quality is easily detected by someone who prefers others above himself (Romans 12:10). It means that true humility can be seen when we are willing to serve others (John 13: 4–17) and to honor people we believe to be less fortunate than we are. The quality of being humble always comes at a price because of the constant need to deny selfish ambitions that are always confronting us. Self-deprecation, lowliness of mind, and freedom from prideful actions are what humility is all about (Job 22:29, Psalm 9:12, Psalm 10:17, Psalm 131:1–2, Proverbs 15:33, Proverbs 27:2, Matthew 5:3, Matthew 20:26, John 13:14–16, Philippians 2:3–11, James 4:6)

Always remember Micah 6:8:

He that has shown thee, O man
What is good, and what doth the Lord require of thee,
But to do justly, and to love mercy,
And to walk humbly with thy God?

5. *Worship* (Matthew 8:2–4)

The word *worship* is literally the act of paying homage to a deity with total reverence and humility as the basis for this honor. Worship, therefore, involves prostrating oneself before the deity being honored or falling down in submission to it as well. God's people have always been encouraged to worship the Lord throughout both testaments, especially in the book of Psalms. Worship is an action that should be exclusively reserved for God alone because He is worthy to be praised above everything else. His goodness, mercy, enduring love, and His provision of salvation are all reasons to worship Him, especially when we do not feel like doing it (Luke 17:11–19). When we encounter these times during our walk with the Lord, it then becomes a "sacrifice" of praise. (Hebrew 13:15) in a literal sense, and we must "pay the price" by dying to our selfish ways in order to honor Him through worship (Exodus 20:3, 2 Kings 17:36, 2 Chronicles 7:1, Psalm 27:4, Psalm 100, Psalm 103:1–4, Psalm 107:6–8, Psalm 149, Psalm 150, Luke 17:11–19, Revelation 4:4–11, Revelation 5:10–14).

6. *The Fruit of the Spirit* (Galatians 5:22–23)

Galatians 5:22–23 provide the believer with a character blueprint of someone who has willingly yielded to the "inner workings of the Holy Spirit. The "fruit" (evidence, produce, or result) of the Lord's spirit influences a believer's life and actions so that there will be certain social manifestations in us, which can be attributed to the likeness of God's character. As noted and defined in the graph below:

Fruit	Preachers Outline and Sermon Bible	Tyndale NT Comm. (Definitions Chart Based on BAGD)	Christian Character Index by Dr. M. Zigarelli
"Agapē" 1. *Love*	Agape love is the love of the mind, of the reason, and of the will. It is basically selfless love.	(None given)	Compassion: A sympathy for the plight of others, especially for the poor.
"Chara" 2. *Joy*	An inner gladness, a deep-seated pleasure. It is a depth of assurance and confidence that ignites a cheerful heart.	"Joy is something quite independent of outward circumstances" for the Christian. Its source is the Holy Spirit.	Having a daily spirit of rejoicing through all circumstances.

Fruit	Preachers Outline and Sermon Bible	Tyndale NT Comm. (Definitions Chart Based on BAGD)	Christian Character Index by Dr. M. Zigarelli
"Eirēnē" 3. Peace	It means to bind together, to join, to weave together. A person is bound, woven, and joined together with himself and others.	Tranquility	Inner peace: Having a calmness within and a general freedom from anxiety.
"Makrōthumia" 4. Patience	Patience, bearing and suffering a long time, perseverance, being constant, steadfast, enduring (longsuffering).	Long tempered, tolerance, putting up with other people, forbearance with others.	Composed tolerance of and response to delay, insult, trouble, or unmet expectations.
"Chrēstotēs" 5. Kindness	It is being kind and good, useful and helpful, gentle and sweet, considerate and gracious through all situations no matter the circumstances.	Goodness or generosity	Acting benevolently and charitably toward others reflected in part by sacrifice of both time and money.
"Agathōsynē" 6. Goodness	It is being full of virtue and excellence, kindness and helpfulness, peace and consideration.	Generosity	Gratitude: The feeling of thankful appreciation for blessings received from God. Habitual focus on what you have rather than what you do not have.

Fruit	Preachers Outline and Sermon Bible	Tyndale NT Comm. (Definitions Chart Based on BAGD)	Christian Character Index by Dr. M. Zigarelli
"Pistis" 7. *Faithfulness*	It means to be faithful and trustworthy, to be loyal and steadfast in devotion and allegiance. It means to be constant, staunch, and enduring.	Faithfulness (NEB, fidelity) Reliability	Commitment to pursue God's will for your life.
"Prätēs" 8. *Gentleness*	It means to be gentle, tender, humble, mild, considerate but strongly so. Meekness has the strength to control and discipline, and it does so at the right time.	Humility	Forgiveness: the willingness to restore others to their original condition, giving up the right to be angry with them.
"Enkrateia" 9. *Self-Control*	To master and control the body or the flesh with all its lusts. It means self-control, the master of desire, appetite, and passion, especially sensual urges and cravings. To be strong and controlled and restrained.[40]	Self-control in sexual matters.[41]	Having the power to control impulses, especially in the use of your tongue, in sexual relationships, in the use of alcohol in what you choose to look at, and in your private thought life.[42]

---

[40] *The Preacher's Outline Sermon Bible—Galatians.* King: Christian Publishers and Ministries, 1991.

[41] *Tyndale New Testament Commentaries—Galatians.* R. Alan Cole, ed. Grand Rapids: Eerdmans Publishing, 1997.

[42] Michael. Zigarelli, *Christian Character Index.* Fairfax: Xulon Press, 2002.

All of these Christlike virtues can only be revealed in a person who willingly yields to the Holy Spirit's leading, while submitting their heart and mind to the Lord. Character virtues of the Holy Spirit are accessed as we allow His transformational power to dominate our spirit and soul for the purpose of obtaining Christ's image (2 Corinthians 3:18).

7. *Displaying a Servant's Heart* (John 13)

The foundation of the Christian faith is based on our ability to follow Christ's example of service found throughout the gospels. He stands as the ultimate model of what a servant ought to be and do. Christ's heart of a servant made it possible for Him to give His best despite the natural and spiritual forces always working against Him. Likewise, believers are expected to serve God and others with the same passion and convictions as Jesus. In order to do this, it will require us to totally empty our egos of self-importance and seek to serve others with a pure heart. In John 13, Jesus builds for us a sure foundation of how to serve by washing the disciple's feet. Here, He willingly takes on the role of a servant-waiter where He humbles Himself by doing one of the most menial tasks in the ancient world. If our Lord was able to perform such a ministry of love and service, how much more should we?

Serving people is where we can learn humility, excellence, brokenness, and respect for authority. Faithfulness is also a very important quality in the life of the one who serves because this is what will qualify this person to go to the "next level" of service when promoted. We must "pay the price" of service before we expect the Lord to fully bless us and advance our ministry effectiveness. Our ability to deny ourselves is how the anointing of the Holy Spirit will grow within our life and ministry (Genesis 29:9–30, Genesis 39:1–6, Exodus 3:1–2, 1 Samuel 16:19–23, 2 Kings 2:1–7).

Finally, in examining the life of Elisha the Prophet, we see his commitment to "pay the price" for the anointing, which he received as a result of his serving Elijah the Prophet.

1 KINGS 19:16–21 AND 2 KINGS 19–22

- Elisha is appointed to succeed Elijah.
- Elisha leaves his occupation to follow Elijah.
- Elijah's mantle (symbol of anointing and authority) is cast upon Elisha.
- Elisha dissolves his earthly ties (mother and father).
- Elisha provides for his family and friends, then leaves with Elijah.
- Elisha continues to follow and serve Elijah from place to place.

2 KINGS 1:3–18

- Elijah (and Elisha) confronts the messengers of King Ahaziah by calling down fire from heaven.

After Elisha served alongside Elijah for a time, he is now given an opportunity to leave his and go on his own. The bond, which had been created, ultimately forged an unusual relationship between the two men. Due to Elisha's faithful service to Elijah, he became qualified to receive a "double portion" (or the birthright inheritance), which belonged to the eldest or firstborn son in a family or ministry. Elisha "paid the price" of self-denial by constantly performing many menial tasks for Elijah that now qualified him to receive a "double portion," be launched into his own ministry, and to receive his "father's or mentor's" blessing. Here is a list of events, which help to confirm the reality of this transference into Elisha's life and ministry.

2 KINGS 2: 1–25

- Elisha is tested in his faithfulness to the call to serve Elijah (Gilgal, Bethel, Jericho, and Jordan).
- Elijah and Elisha experience a miracle by the parting of the Jordan River.
- Elijah asks Elisha, "What can he do for him?" Elisha responds by asking for a "double portion" (the firstborn

blessing/inheritance) to be given to him. It could only be granted if Elijah was truly regarded as Elisha's spiritual Father (see vs. 2 Kings 2:12, "My Father, My Father"), thus signifying that he was indeed a spiritual son in the ministry. Elisha sees the chariot of fire take Elijah away and his desire is granted.

- Elisha takes Elijah's mantle (an example of his ministry anointing) and begins his own ministry of miracles.
- Elisha smites the Jordan River and duplicates Elijah's miracle.
- The sons of the prophets confirm that Elisha has received of his master's anointing as they bow to him.
- The sons of the prophets do not fully believe that Elijah has left, and that Elisha is their new mentor/leader.
- Elisha heals the water supply with salt.
- Elisha's authority is established after the death of some young men who mocked him.

2 KINGS 3: 11–15

- Elisha is sought by King Jehoshaphat in order to inquire of the Lord.
- Elisha asks for a musician to be brought to him so that the presence of the Lord could become present.

2 KINGS 4:1–44

- Elisha multiplies the widow's oil in order to pay her debt.
- The Shunamite's son is raised from the dead by Elisha.
- Elisha makes a poisonous meal safe to eat.
- Food is miraculously multiplied and much is left for another day.

2 KINGS 5:1–27

- Naaman the Leper is healed by washing in the Jordan River seven times.

- Elisha's servant, Gehazi, is discovered to be a liar and a person of greed. He no longer is qualified to be mentored by Elisha.

2 KINGS 6:1–33 AND 7:1–20

- The miracle of the floating ax-head.
- Elisha warns the King of Israel of the Syrians plan of attack.
- The king of Syria pursues Elisha because of his warning the king of Israel of his plan. They encompass Elisha at Dothan and try to take his by force. Elisha's servant panics, but Elisha assures him of the Lord's supernatural angelic presence for their safety. The pursuers are smitten with blindness.
- The famine in Samaria and Elisha's prophecy concerning it.

2 KINGS 8: 1–15 AND 2 KINGS 9: 1–37

- Elisha's prophecy for the Shunamite woman's destiny concerning the famine.
- Elisha informs the king of Syria of his death and of Hazael's appointment to be king of Syria.
- Elisha sends one of his servants to anoint Jehu to be king of Israel and to kill Joram.

2 KINGS 13: 14–21

- Elisha's ministry comes to an end by his death after he prophesied the defeat of the king of Syria by the hand of Joash.
- Elisha's bones revive a dead soldier.

Every manifestation of the Holy Spirit's anointing in Elisha's life can be directly attributed to his servant's heart, obedience to the Lord, previous ministry training, and a willingness to "pay the price" for this costly anointing. We have seen throughout this book that the Spirit's anointing comes at a price and is increased at a price. God's grace must not be taken for granted, nor should we expect it to be free of our personal sacrifice.

Devotionals

The following devotionals have been designed to complement the preceding study on the anointing of the Holy Spirit. There are many ways for a believer to enhance the anointing of God within their life. This can be accomplished by selecting and practicing the devotionals that suit their personal style of interacting with the Holy Spirit. It is recommended that at least two or three devotionals be practiced each month in order to maximize the benefit of each spiritual discipline.

Devotional 1

———— ❧ ————

Be Filled with the Holy Spirit

*Then Peter said unto them, repent, and be baptized every
one of you in the name of Jesus Christ for the remission of
sins, and ye shall receive the gift of the Holy Ghost.*

—*Acts 2:38*

The disciples of Jesus were instructed by Him to wait in Jerusalem
for the coming promise of the Holy Spirit. One hundred and
twenty believers heeded these words and waited in an upper room
until the Spirit was poured out on every one of them. Christ's death,
burial, and resurrection now made it possible for the Holy Spirit to
come and indwell the hearts of all who called Jesus Lord and Savior.

The provision for man's salvation, sanctification, and deliverance had been accomplished by the shedding of Jesus's blood on the
cross, and this cleansing made it possible for all believers to receive
the Holy Spirit's initial justification. This led to our ability to experience the fullness of the indwelling of the Holy Spirit as the second
step in our transformation and empowerment for ministry service
to the Lord. Receiving the baptism of the Holy Spirit, as we have
already discussed, is the reception of God's anointing for holiness,
sanctification, and service to Him. Once received, we now possess
the same power Christ had when He walked the earth and performed
many miracles. The same anointing had been given to the Church in

order to duplicate the same ministry of Christ, but we must seek after this wonderful provision as a starving man seeks to have his hunger and thirst quenched.

This imagery can be supported by Isaiah 55:1, which highlights the desperate plight of the buyer seeking to have these two basic needs met, hunger and thirst. If there is no seeking, then we can't expect the Lord to meet our needs as declared throughout the scriptures (Jeremiah 29:13, Matthew 7:7, Luke 11:9). In John 7:37–38, Jesus lays out the formula clearly for all to see when he says, *"If any man thirst, let him come unto me, and drink."* The thought here is that of seeking and going after Jesus as the supplier of the Holy Spirit (the anointing). The promise results in our being filled with "rivers of living water (that being an endless supply of the Holy Spirit's anointing) if we would simply humble ourselves and ask for this experience. Jesus died and rose again to provide the gift of salvation and the Holy Spirit for all who would be followers of Him; therefore, the Church must once again visit its foundation in spirituality if it will have a chance to impact this current generation (see Acts 2:39, 19:1–6, Ephesians 5:18).

Reflection Questions

1. Have I been *filled* with the Holy Spirit?
2. When is the last time I have sought the Lord for more of his Spirit in my life?
3. Is the fruit of the Spirit (Galatians 5:22–23) evident in my life?
4. Do I see a need for more of the Holy Spirit's role in my handling of everyday events?

Spiritual Practices

1. Try taking a few days to research throughout the Bible the topic of the Holy Spirit.
2. Plan to take at least two days to reflect on where you are spiritually and then journal about your findings.

3. Find time to pray every morning for about fifteen minutes as you ask the Holy Spirit to fill up for the day's journey ahead.

Devotional 2

Be Studious

Study to show thyself approved unto God, a
workman that needeth not to be ashamed,
rightly dividing the word or truth.

—*2 Timothy 2:15*

The foundation for spiritual growth in the Lord will always be found in the reading and studying of scripture. The Bible or Word of God is a believer's source of strength, peace, joy, power, and conviction to live out their life in Christ to the max. Regularly seeking to understand God and His ways can be found by reading of the various characters and events, which are displayed throughout both the Old and New Testaments. This information helps to guide the believer on their journey of maturing in the Lord as they put into practice the principles, precepts, statutes, and commandments expressed in scripture.

Once we have become skilled in the knowledge and personal application of biblical truth, then we can expect to have a deeper encounter with God through the Holy Spirit. This encounter should include a greater revelation of the scriptures, the ability to make God-centered decisions in wisdom, an overall ability to reason biblical truths with others, an evidence of spiritual maturity (see Galatians

5:22–23), and the ability to produce an authentic anointing of power by the word and Spirit working together within us.

One of the main benefits of studying the Bible is that it provides fuel to the Holy Spirit's fire, which burns in the hearts of those who are genuinely seeking the Lord for more of His presence and power. It is the Word of God that works in conjunction with the Holy Spirit to produce an anointing to set the captive free (Isaiah 10:27), and it is the person who is willing to give Himself to the study of the scriptures who will capture this awesome benefit from the Lord.

Here are a few biblical passages, which can be very useful for the student who desires a deeper walk with the Lord: Psalms 119:130, 119:105, 119:133, 119:11, 119:9, Psalm 37:31, Isaiah 40:8, Psalm 107:20, Matthew 4:4, John 15:7, 17:17, 1:1, 14, Hebrews 4:12, Revelation 12:11.

All of these texts will serve the serious student in their pursuit of truth as they seek to purify and maintain a vibrant life with the Lord Jesus Christ.

Reflection Questions

1. How often do I read the Word of God for my daily sustenance?
2. Do I read the Word of God seeking to be transformed by its truth and content?
3. What are you looking for while reading the Word of God, understanding, information, guidance, peace, the revelation of truth, or to simply commune with the Lord?
4. Am I reading for quantity or quality of divine truth?

Spiritual Practices

1. Try doing a *topical study* from the Word of God on something of interest to you.
2. Try reading an entire book of the Bible and extract key points you feel relate to where you are in your current walk with the Lord.

3. Read all the parables of Jesus and let them speak to your heart.
4. Try listening to a pastor's next sermon or Bible study and take notes which you can use for your private devotional time during that week.

Devotional 3

— ◦◦◦ —

Be Teachable

And seeing the multitudes, he went up into a mountain:
and when he was set, his disciples came unto him:
And he opened his mouth, and taught them...

—Matthew 5:1–2

I n this scripture, the disciple Matthew recalls how Jesus intentionally gathered the twelve together for formal training and debriefing
for his sermons and ministry events. Jesus was a committed teacher
who sought to bring the law and other historical portions of the Old
Testament to light as He interpreted His Father's purpose throughout His ministry. In like manner, believers are expected to study,
search, and apply biblical truth to their everyday lives with the hope
of becoming transformed into Christ's image (Romans 12:2).

Our willingness to be taught by others is a real sign of humility
and a hunger for more truth. In order for believers to be properly
educated in the scriptures, Ephesians 4:11 ministers have been given
to the Church, as well as the Holy Spirit who is called "alongside"
us to reveal truth beyond what mankind can each us (John 14:26).
It is the Holy Spirit who can enlighten hidden meanings found in
God's word and brings revelation to many misunderstood passages
of scripture. When this occurs in our lives, we are then able to grow
and mature in Christ at a rapid rate and then be released to operate

in various levels of power and authority through the anointing of the Holy Spirit.

Remember, we are commanded in 2 Timothy 2:15 to study the word of God so that we are able to "rightly divide" its truths. This process begins once we are able to submit ourselves to good teachers who are committed to the teaching of sound doctrine (teaching, 2 Timothy 4:3). We can then begin to grow in faith, power, character, and the grace of God.

Reflection Questions

1. How often do you study what you have been taught during the week?
2. Have you thought about teaching others what you have been learning?
3. Have you ever done a book-by-book study of Jesus's teachings beginning in the book of Matthew?
4. What have you learned about God over the past three months?

Spiritual Practices

1. Learn all you can about the beatitudes of Jesus (Matthew 5, 6, 7).
2. Do an extensive study on the parables of Jesus.
3. Seek to do some topical studies on salvation, the covenants of God, the fruit of the Spirit (Galatians 5:22–23), spiritual gifts, and miracles of Jesus.
4. Ask someone to evaluate your teachability and attitude while being taught.

Devotional 4

— ✑ —

Meditation

This book of the law shall not depart out of thy mouth:
but thou shalt meditate therein day and night,
that thou mayest observe to do according to all that is written therein:
for then thou shalt make thy way prosperous,
and then thou shalt have good success.

—Joshua 1:8

The individual who is going to be a person used under the anointing of the Holy Spirit will be the person who learns to meditate on the Word of God. In Hebrew, the word *meditate* (H7742) means to muse (put forth thoughts), commune, speak, complain or (H1897) to ponder, muse, imagine, devise; to murmur, to talk, or study. The ability to meditate on or to ponder the principles of the scriptures is a valuable skill in the life of a believer. When we focus on something to the point that we create a visible image in our mind of the thing desired, we are actually giving life through our thoughts. This is actually what meditation can accomplish. With this, an individual has learned how to internalize the principles and truths revealed in scripture by meditating morning and evening as Joshua 1:8 declares. Our ability to ponder and focus on what we have both read and heard makes all the difference in the world because we have allowed what we have read to actually read us. By meditating on the scriptures, we can now begin to have the Holy Spirit reveal powerful truth, which can in turn make us free. By meditating or pondering God's Word, we can now build within us a mental picture through our imagination that can become a force for an overcoming life in Christ. We are what we think about and ponder every single day, resulting in either a life of victory or one of defeat. God reminded Joshua that his success would be founded upon his ability to successfully meditate (to ponder) and confess His word all day long.

The power of the anointing can be found throughout both testaments as revealed in God's dealings with His people and leaders. It's the Lord's word that empowers us to accomplish His will as we allow it to build strength within us (see Isaiah 55:10–11). Through meditation, we learn to think like God thinks, which ultimately leads us to act like He acts. The Apostle Paul recognizes this when He encourages the believers at Philippi when He says, "Think on these things" (Philippians 4:8–9) as opposed to other things. Remember, the overall principle of meditation, "For as a man thinketh in his heart, so is he" (Proverbs 23:7).

Reflection Questions

1. When is the last time you made it a priority to memorize scripture?
2. What thoughts have recently dominated your thinking, and why?
3. What Bible passages mean the most to you?
4. Do you feel the Lord's presence while reading the scriptures?

Spiritual Practices
Additional key scriptures to explore on this subject:

- Psalm 1:2, Psalm 63:6, Psalm 77:12
- Psalm 119:15, 23, 48, 78, and 148
- Psalm 143:5—"I remember the days of old; I meditate on ally thy work; I muse on the work of thy hands."
- 1 Timothy 4:15

1. Memorize Psalm 23 in its entirety.
2. Meditate on the latest events in your life and allow God to speak to your heart through a Bible passage.
3. Read the book of Ecclesiastes and ponder its contents.
4. Practice meditating on what the Lord has done in your life over the past few months.

Devotional 5

Be Prayerful

Pray without ceasing.

—1 Thessalonians 5:17

The believer had always been encouraged to seek after the Lord in prayer because it is the very foundation of Christian service to God. Everything we say and do should be a by-product of our communing with the Lord for insight, direction, strength, and faith for our long journey ahead. A person seeking the anointing of the Holy Spirit will always find himself petitioning God in prayer for more of His love and power to accomplish the ministry assigned to them. Jesus was often found praying early in the morning so He could be undistracted in His quest to know His Father's will for that particular day. Likewise, we must hunger to know our heavenly Father's plan for our lives daily if we are going to find fulfillment and purpose in life. Prayer is simply communication with God by use of words or thoughts as we then wait to hear His voice on a given matter we presented to Him. The more we pray, the greater our fellowship and relationship will be with the Lord. We begin to grow as the evidence of this union becomes apparent to others (Matthew 6:6).

When Jesus was asked by His disciples about prayer, He responded by sharing with them a model for how to pray effectively in Matthew 6:9–13, which says,

1. *Our Father,* signifying that the Lord not only hears our prayer as His children, but every person in covenant with Him should expect Him to meet their desires and petitions.
2. *Which art in heaven,* the Lord is able to help us overcome any problem because of His perspective and geographical position, which is in heaven!
3. *Hallowed be thy name,* the Lord's name is to be worshipped and praised *before* we start petitioning Him.
4. *Thy kingdom come,* the king's domain belongs to Jesus Christ and fellow believers, and we are to pray heaven's reality into existence on the earth.
5. *Thy will be done on earth,* God's desire must manifest here on earth.
6. *Give us this day our daily bread,* just like the children of Israel received manna (daily bread) from the Lord as their provider, so are we to ask for his provision daily.
7. *And forgive us our debts, as we forgive our debtors,* if our prayers are to be answered, we need to forgive people who have trespassed against us.
8. *And lead us not into temptation,* we now ask the Lord to keep (preserve) us from the temptation to sin.
9. *But deliver us from evil,* or more literally "deliver us from the evil one," who is Satan.
10. *For thine is the kingdom,* the kingdom is the Lord's and His alone. (The kingdom is not the Church, heaven, or the people of the earth but includes them all.)
11. *And the power,* Jesus said, "All power is given unto me in heaven and in earth," thus pointing to His superiority over all creation. This explosive dynamic power emanates from God Himself through the Holy Spirit.
12. *And the glory, forever,* all honor, praise, and glory belongs to the Lord, so why don't we bless His holy name.

Jesus's blueprint for effective and successful prayer was given to His disciples then and now. We should take the time to rehearse these components during our time of study so that prayer will become much more fruitful (Numbers 21:7, Genesis 32:9–11, 2 Chronicles 7:14, Psalm 5:3, 17:1, 54:2, 102:1–2, John 17, Acts 31, 16:25–26).

Reflection Questions

1. How much quality time do you spend with God in prayer?
2. What types of prayers have you learned to offer to the Lord?
3. Do you find yourself praying more about your needs, or the needs of others?
4. Have you ever practiced the "power-side" of prayer, which is simply listening for a response from the Lord after you have petitioned him?

Spiritual Practices

1. Try practicing Jesus's model of prayer in Matthew 6:5–15 and see how it effects your life during a four-week period of time.
2. Enlist a prayer partner who has a deep conviction about their commitment to prayer as often as possible.
3. Take two nights a week and intercede on behalf of others to resolve personal situations and world problems.
4. Build a devotional life, which includes a song of worship, a scripture verse to remember, prayer, and finally giving thanks to God in advance for his answer to prayer.

Devotional 6

―― ✑ ――

Walk in Love

Be ye therefore followers of God, as dear children;
and walk in love, as Christ also hath loved us,
and hath given himself for us an offering and a sacrifice
to God for a sweet-smelling savor.

—Ephesians 5:1–2

One of the primary focuses of the Bible is the topic of love. God's love for us. Our love for God and man's love for each other. There are countless examples in both testaments that illustrate negative and positive interactions of people trying to maintain a love relationship. Cain and Abel, God and Adam, David and Saul, along with the many stories and parables of Jesus. Our struggle is with becoming vulnerable to people we say that we love and with reconciling our feelings with those who have hurt us. The Bible deals with this dilemma by giving us a pure example of godly love found in 1 Corinthians 13:1–13. In this text, we find what love truly is because the Apostle Paul gives us a detailed breakdown of what love actually looks like. He says it:

- Suffers long, is kind
- Does not envy
- It vaunteth not itself

- Is not puffed up
- Does not behave itself unseemly
- Seeketh not her own
- Is not easily provoked
- Thinketh no evil
- Does not rejoice in iniquity
- Bears all things
- Believeth all things
- Hopeth all things
- Endureth all things
- Never fails

These fourteen characteristics of love are timeless qualities believers are expected to possess and exhibit as they interact within society and each other. Love overlooks the faults of others and is determined to see the good in people. If we are going to be used to do anointed ministry, it must be founded on intense love for people. The scriptures tell us of how Jesus was "moved with compassion" (Matthew 9:36, 14:14, 15:32, 20:34, Mark 1:41, 5:19, 6:34, 9:22, Luke 7:13), which can be interpreted as "pity, sympathy, or to have the bowels yearn" according to Strong's Concordance. All of these feelings are based upon a heart that is fixed in its love for people. The power and anointing of the Holy Spirit moves best when motivated by love and compassion. Let us always seek to "walk in love."

Reflection Questions

1. What are the top five people or things you can say that you truly love?
2. Next, evaluate the order in which they appear, and why?
3. Are there any hindrances in your life, which you think might prevent you from loving others?
4. What ways do you choose to show God, your neighbors, and family that you love them?

Spiritual Practices

1. Donate a financial gift to a need-based organization for the next three months.
2. Do a good deed for one of your neighbors.
3. Serve one Saturday a month for the next two months at a hospital, goodwill center, homeless shelter, or AIDS ward.
4. Make it a point to walk in love by forgiving someone who has offended you by talking to them and resolving the disagreement.

Devotional 7

---❦---

The Power of Fasting

*Is not this the fast that I have chosen? To loose the bands
of wickedness, to undo the heavy burdens, and to let the
oppressed go free, and that ye break every yoke?'*

—*Isaiah 58:6*

The Bible often talks about fasting in both testaments because it was a common occurrence among God's people. Fasting in the Old Testament was usually done in conjunction with repentance when Israel failed to obey the laws of God or when they needed His help to overcome an enemy (see 1 Samuel 7:6, 2 Samuel 12:16–20, Nehemiah 1:4, Esther 4:16). In the New Testament, believers often fasted to be empowered for Christian service or to know the will of God (Acts 13:1–3, 2 Corinthians 6:4–5). The main purpose of fasting is to draw closer to the Lord by the humbling of body and soul. This can be accomplished as we deny ourselves of various pleasures and appetites of the flesh. Abstinence from food, conversation, or anything that would seek to dominate our thought-life could qualify as a deterrent against our fleshly desires.

Isaiah 58 gives us a wonderful picture of what fasting can accomplish. The prophet Isaiah reminds us that fasting does not make God do what we want, guarantee that we are drawn closer to God, or that we become instantly humbled before God, but it does reveal our heart's attitude toward life. Our motives must be pure if we are going to gain an answer to prayer or deliverance from a heavy burden because God is always interested in teaching us something as we transition through the event. The question you may be asking is, "What are some benefits of fasting?"

1. We have better self-control.
2. We can quiet our fleshy desires.
3. We diminish the natural craving for food.
4. We have a greater capacity to love our enemies (Psalm 35:11–14).
5. We become more open for the anointing of the Holy Spirit.
6. We become more compassionate to the needs of people around the world.
7. We receive more time to hear the voice of God clearly.
8. We become a conduit for the power of the Holy Spirit to destroy "yokes and heavy burdens" (Isaiah 10:27).
9. Remember: more love, more power!

Reflection Questions

1. Have you ever used fasting as a means to deny yourself of worldly pleasure?
2. List several reasons why you feel you need to fast.
3. Do you see fasting as a means to acquiring more spiritual power from the Lord?
4. Have you tried fasting for one to two days and then kept a journal of your experience or perhaps to record what the Lord spoke to your heart?

Spiritual Practices

1. Fast one day a week for twelve or twenty-four hours and record what happens.
2. Abstain from watching TV, listening to the radio, or using the internet for one day a week.

3. During your personal fast, try establishing a pattern of worship, Bible study, and prayer over the course of your period of consecration.

4. Read *Celebration of Discipline* by Richard Foster or *God's Chosen Fast* by Arthur Wallis.

Devotional 8

Praying in the Spirit

I thank my God, I speak with tongues more than ye all.

—*1 Corinthians 14:18*

The greatest gift given to the Church is the Holy Spirit because of His ability to empower and guide believers into effective ministry for Christ. Jesus promised the coming of the Spirit in John 14:16–17, 16:17–11, and this promise found its fulfillment in Acts 2:1–4 where it was poured out on the hundred and twenty in the upper room. As the believers were praying and seeking the Lord, suddenly the spirit of God filled every believer and they began to "speak with other tongues" (Acts 2:4). The followers of Jesus finally received this precious possession, which would not only assist them in fulfilling the Great Commission (Matthew 28:18–20) but also provide a means for activating the dimension of spiritual realities. This gift made it possible for human beings to be used to impact heaven and earth for the glory of God (Luke 10:1–20, Mark 16:15–20, Acts 1:8). Receiving the baptism of the Holy Spirit is the key to operating in the supernatural; therefore, this empowerment must be highly sought after if we want to duplicate the ministry of Christ (John 14:12).

The Apostle Paul has a clear understanding of this mandate from our Lord, and he often reminded believers to be "filled with the Spirit" (Ephesians 5:18) and to pray in the Spirit (or in tongues). In fact, he was so persuaded that praying in the Spirit (tongues) was the right thing to do, that he boasted about it by saying, "I thank my God, I speak with tongues more than ye all" (1 Corinthians 14:8). Paul acknowledges his being filled with the Spirit and his ability to speak in tongues. He knows that by using his prayer language (tongues), he can access God's spiritual dimension much easier. Jude, the brother of James, echoes Paul's instruction by saying, "But you, beloved, building yourselves up on your most Holy faith; *praying in the Holy Spirit*." Once again, we can see how important it is for believers to pray using their prayer language as much as possible. It literally helps to "build up" the spirit of the person praying and enlarges their capacity for more of the Holy Spirit's presence in their lives. Another important benefit to praying in the Spirit is that the Holy Spirit actually influences our prayers as we seek to intercede on behalf of others. Romans 8:26–27 suggests this by saying, "*Likewise the Spirit also helpeth our infirmities: for we know not what we should pray for as we ought: but the Spirit itself maketh intercession for us with groanings which cannot be uttered. And he that searcheth the hearts knoweth what is the mind of the Spirit, because he maketh intercession for the saints according to the will of God.*"

The above scripture confirms the fact that the Holy Spirit prays through us and for us when we intercede for others, and this experience ushers us into the presence, purpose, and power of the Spirit. Finally, praying in the Spirit (tongues) is quite simply the doorway into the supernatural. If believers are going to deepen their walk in the Spirit, they must learn to exercise the gift of tongues on a daily basis.

Reflection Questions

1. Have you ever received the gift of the Holy Spirit as understood in Acts 2:4?
2. If you are filled with the Holy Spirit, how often do you pray in the Spirit (or tongues) during the week?

3. What method(s) do you use to enhance the anointing of the Holy Spirit within your life? Is it worship, studying scripture, praying in tongues, etc...?

Spiritual Practices

1. Try praying in the Spirit (tongues) for to thirty minutes in the morning.
2. Try interceding for others by using the Holy Spirit as mentioned in Romans 8:26–27.
3. Try singing in the Spirit as mentioned in Ephesians 5:19 ("spiritual songs") to the song *I Love You Lord* or *I Exalt Thee* as you sing in tongues while using the melody of one of these songs.
4. Read books, which emphasize the baptism of the Holy Spirit and speaking in tongues.

Devotional 9

---- ❦ ----

Fellowship

And they continued steadfastly in the apostles' doctrine and
fellowship, and in breaking of bread, and in prayers.

—Acts 2:42

The Greek word for fellowship is *koinonia*, which means communion, distribution, (social) intercourse, partnership, and almsgiving. *Koinonia's* essential meaning is that of partnership, which is
based on a communal relationship of peace. Early church believers
were expected to have an ongoing relationship with the Lord and
fellow saints as they tried to build on both of these relationships
(the fellowship of believers with each other and with the Lord). In
fact, Holy Communion (the table of the Lord) was a sacrament of
the church, which embodied this two-fold relationship as believers
remembered the body and blood of the Lord (1 Corinthians. 10:16–
17, 11:23–32, Matthew 26:26–29). This partnership was expected
to transcend the communion table by having believers share their
material wealth and resources with others (Romans 15:26–27, 2
Corinthians 8:4, 9:13, and Philippians 1:5, 4:15). The bearing of
one another's burdens (Romans 15:1, Galatians 6:2), as well as the
sufferings (2 Corinthians 1:7, Philippians 1:7) of others. This is the
more practical aspect of *koinonia* (partnership); believers are encouraged to experience with each other.

A more profound truth revealed in scripture concerning *koinonia* (partnership, fellowship) is in an Old Testament example of Saul fellowshipping among the prophets (1 Samuel 10:11–12). Through the power of this partnership, King Saul, who was not a prophet, began to exhibit the anointing of a prophet because of his being in the company (partnership) of prophetic individuals. Here we can learn an important principle: "association brings on assimilation." Thus, we become like those whom we build partnerships with over time. King Saul for a limited period functioned under a prophetic anointing, which allowed him to prophesy as a formally trained prophet. A New Testament example is found in Acts 2:1 where it says, *"And when the day of Pentecost was fully come, they were all with one accord in one place."*

This verse highlights the depth of unity, oneness, fellowship, and partnership working harmoniously to bring about the Holy Spirit's presence in the upper room. The main idea here is that of *koinonia* being the unifying factor within a community of believers. When we come together in unity, we can expect the Holy Spirit to be there with us as stated in Acts 2:2–4 and Psalm 133:1–3. It should be noted that the anointing of the Holy Spirit manifests itself when believers are on one accord and at peace with each other. Our prayer must be like Christ's in John 17:11, 21–23 that pleads with believers to endeavor to remain one in relationship to Him and each other. Fellowship with God and others is essential to personal growth and development toward spiritual and social maturity. May we begin to prioritize better interaction between the Lord and fellow believers.

Reflection Questions

1. How often do you seek to fellowship with other believers?
2. Do you consider social fellowship to be a valid part of evangelism?
3. How much time do you spend in fellowship with the Lord in prayer and worship during the week?
4. Have you joined a Christian group or ministry that will help you to be accountable in your walk with the Lord?

Spiritual Practices

1. Meet with a friend once a week for an accountability session.
2. Prioritize your attendance at every church service this year.
3. Become actively involved in your church by participating in a volunteer ministry for one year.
4. Commit yourself to receiving the sacrament of Holy Communion, which embodies true fellowship.

Devotional 10

— ✑ —

Praise and Worship

Enter his gates with thanksgiving,
and into his courts with praise: be thankful unto him,
and bless his name. For the Lord is good; his mercy is everlasting
and his truth endureth to all generations.

—Psalm 100:4–5

The scriptures are filled with numerous exhortations to praise and worship the Lord. The word *praise* can be defined as an expression of approval, esteem, or commendation, while worship can simply mean to bow down (prostrate) in homage to something or someone. These terms provide a glimpse into the actions of someone who is expected to be a person honoring God. If believers learn some of the proper ways for glorifying Him, they will begin to experience more of the benefits associated with praising the Lord (Psalms 22:3, 67:3–7, 100:1–5, 103:1–22, 105:1–45, 107:1–43, 126:1–6, 137:1–9, 149, 150). A good example of just how powerful worship can be is found in 2 Chronicles 5:13, where it is recorded how the musicians and singers were of one heart to bless the name of the Lord in Solomon's temple. The passage says, *"The trumpeters and singers were as one, to make one sound to be heard in praising and thanking the Lord; and when they lifted up their voice with the trumpeters and cymbals and instruments of music, and praised the Lord, saying. For he is good; for his mercy endureth for ever: that then the house was filled with a cloud, even the house of the Lord…"*

The presence of the Holy Spirit was so powerful that it prevented the priests from completing their ministry responsibilities within the house of the Lord (see vs. 14). When God's people understand how important it is to worship and praise the Lord with purity of heart, we can expect the presence of God to be in rich abundance. Therefore, without proper knowledge of the purpose of praise and worship, believers may be in danger of offering superficial worship to a worthy Lord (see Jeremiah 7:2–7). If our full attention is only on the Lord and not "other gods," we should anticipate a rich outpouring of the Holy Spirit that comes to increase the anointing of God.

Singing and praising the Lord is a vital part of our existence because we were created to worship and to honor our Creator. In fact, when we get to heaven, the redeemed will be joined by the angelic host in worshipping the Lamb who sits upon the throne. Revelation 4–5 paints a wonderful picture of what the worship atmosphere will be like for eternity. While we are still here on earth, we need to prepare our hearts and minds for what eventually awaits us in heaven. Our desire must be to set time aside from our busy schedules and praise the Lord for what he has done and worship Him for who He is. If we want more of an anointing upon our personal ministries, we have to seek the Lord while He can be found (Jeremiah 29:11–14).

Reflection Questions

1. Do I praise the Lord in private and in public when given the opportunity?
2. Do you enjoy personal time with the Lord in quiet intimate fellowship?
3. Have you discovered the power of worship by experiencing the outpouring of the Holy Spirit's anointing upon you?
4. Do you believe that the giving of your time to the Lord, or the giving of finances is a part of your worship experience?

Spiritual Practices

1. Take thirty minutes to privately worship and praise the Lord.
2. Listen to music that is centered in worship and then listen to the Holy Spirit. (Allow Him to speak to you.)
3. Try attending a church worship service different from what you know.
4. Praise, worship, pray, and then wait to sense the Holy Spirit's anointing and presence.

Devotional 11

Hearing the Voice of the Lord

My sheep hear my voice, and I know them, and they follow me.

—*John 10:27*

Hearing the voice of the Lord is of great necessity for believers that desire to grow closer to God. This can be accomplished by either reading the written word of God to discern his voice or by listening to the voice of the Holy Spirit. Since we have already covered studying the word of God in an earlier chapter, I would like to focus on the need to hear the voice of God by the Spirit. The Lord has always desired to speak to His people directly (Genesis 1:29–30, Exodus 3:4–10, Genesis 6:13–22) or by the mouths of His prophets (Isaiah 1:1–4, Ezekiel 2:1–8, Jeremiah 2:1–20). The focus of this study is to encourage the believer to hear the voice of the Lord for themselves. Jesus said, "My sheep hear my voice," thus indicating that Christ's followers are expected to cultivate their ability to hear His voice. This can be done by

1. praying and then waiting to hear the Holy Spirit speak back to you,
2. understanding how and why God speaks to us by studying the prophetic books of the Bible,

3. reading Bible-centered curriculum on "*how to hear the voice of God,*"
4. practicing the presence of God by being silent and secluded for thirty minutes a day, and
5. understanding that the voice of God is usually heard as a "still small voice" (1 Kings 19:9–12) and not a thunderous booming noise.

It is very important to understand that hearing the voice of God is usually followed up by an anointing from the Lord in order to empower someone for ministry service (Moses, Exodus 7:8–12; Elisha, 1 Kings 19:9–18; Jesus, Matthew 3:16–17; Paul, Acts 9: 1–6). Strength for ministry comes as a result of hearing the Lord's voice, which, in fact, authorizes someone to "go forth" in His name. These individuals are examples of delegated authority and what His voice can empower us to do. Some important guidelines for hearing the voice of the Lord are found in 1 Samuel 3:1–14:

(Vs. 1)—We must be actively involved in *ministry unto the Lord.*

(Vs. 1)—The word of the Lord must be highly esteemed "precious" in our eyes.

(Vs. 2–3)—Know that "old ways" or traditions may hinder what God is trying to do in your life presently.

(Vs. 4–6)—Expect to hear from the Lord and allow mature overseers to assist in your development.

(Vs. 7)—To "know" the Lord is to become intimate with him through fellowship.

(Vs. 8–10)—Test the voice/spirit (1 John 4:1) to see if it is actually the Lord's voice; if so, respond.

(Vs. 11–14)—Hear and understand what the Lord has said to you.

Reflection Questions

1. What was the last thing you believe God spoke to your heart, and why?

2. How much do you seek to know the will of God for your
   life?
3. Are you journaling about what God has been saying to you
   this year?

Spiritual Practices

1. Make a list of the top five topics the Lord has been speaking to you.
2. Read the book of Jeremiah and note the struggles he had
   once he heard the voice of the Lord.
3. For the next five days, try being still while you are alone
   and allow the Lord to speak to you for fifteen to twenty
   minutes per day.

Devotional 12

Humility

But he giveth more grace. Wherefore he saith, God resisteth the proud, but giveth grace unto the humble.

—James 4:6

One of the most desirable virtues a person can have is that of humility. A humble person is one who seeks to prefer others better than himself because they do not see themselves above or greater in status than anyone else. Micah 6:8 states that God requires believers to walk in humility, and He esteems those who are of a humble and contrite spirit as they tremble at His word (Isaiah 66:2). No matter how successful or blessed we become, we must remember that if it had not been for the Lord's goodness, we would have nothing. This kind of self-awareness is always needed if we are going to maintain a vibrant life in Christ and have favor with the Lord.

Pride has always been an opposing force against our Lord as documented in scriptures like Genesis 4:1–16, Exodus 8:28–32, 1 Samuel 18:5–16, Isaiah 14:12–15, Mark 7:21–23 and 1 John 2:16. Perhaps one of the best stories in the entire Bible that speak to this issue is the account of King Nebuchadnezzar's rise and fall because of this pride (Daniel 4:1–37). The king had previously commanded that the three Hebrew young men be put into a fiery furnace because they disobeyed his ordinance. His excessive misuse of authority led him to believe he was more important than he actually was in the sight of God. Therefore, the Lord gave him a dream that needed to be interpreted by his spiritual advisors. No one could interpret the dream except for Daniel, who basically told him that he would cease to be the king for seven years but not lose his throne. Upon losing his mind, the king was driven into the wilderness to live as an animal (vs. 31–33) for an ordained time (vs. 23). He literally became as a beast of the field (vs. 32) until his pride was broken, his mind returned to him (vs. 36), and he learned the lesson of being humble before the Lord (vs. 37). Nebuchadnezzar's ordeal yields many truths, such as:

1. God hates pride (Proverbs 6:16–17).
2. He will orchestrate events in our lives to promote a change-of-heart attitude toward him and others.
3. He "resists the proud but gives grace to the humble."
4. He wants us to walk humbly before him (Micah 6:8).
5. We should learn from other biblical characters who were destroyed for their pride: Asa (2 Chronicles 16), Amaziah (2 Chronicles 25), and Absalom (2 Samuel 13–15).

Finally, we must accept Christ's example of humility (Philippians 2:5–8) as we seek to become servants of all (Mark 9:33–37, John 13:1–17) by submitting ourselves unto God in the likeness of the "servant leader" Jesus our Savior. There is no formula, which guarantees humility, but we can follow Christ as a model of true humility and service to others.

Remember, the anointing of the Holy Spirit moves greatest amongst people who are of a humble heart!

Reflection Questions

1. Do you consider yourself a humble person? If so, what can you say to support your claim?
2. Do you believe other people view you as a person of humility?

3. When you become angry, what do you verbalize or think about the other person?
4. Am I submissive to authority, or do I have to have my own way?

Spiritual Practices

1. Ask a leader in your church if you can serve as a helper within a much-needed ministry over the next four to six weeks.
2. Take a Saturday out of your schedule and do two or three kind activities for one or more of your neighbors (preferably someone you may not know or like).
3. Bless a Christian organization with a substantial financial gift ($100 to $500) without expecting anything in return.
4. Forgive someone who has wronged you over the last two years.

Devotional 13

~ ⌘ ~

Practice, Practice, Practice

*But solid food is for the mature, who because of practice
have their senses trained to discern good and evil.*

—*Hebrews 5:14 NASB*

It has been said that one day, a man asked directions from a stranger
by saying, "How do you get to Carnegie Hall?" The stranger
answered, "Practice, practice, practice." This has been a fundamental
principle for anyone desiring to improve some aspect of their life or
to become a person of excellence. As a musician, I can appreciate the
discipline of practice in order to become a proficient instrumental-
ist. The more I practiced, the more I became one with my instrument and more confident when I played before audiences. The above
scripture highlights this much-forgotten truth, and Matthew Henry
comments on it by saying, "*There are spiritual senses as well as those
that are natural. The soul has its sensations as well as the body; these are
much depraved and lost by sin, but they are recovered by grace. It is by use
an exercise that these senses are improved, made more quick and strong
to taste the sweetness of what is good and true, and the bitterness of what
is false and evil.*"

Essentially, Paul is saying that the person who does not exercise
their physical, mental, and spiritual faculties will most likely not be
able to mature in Christ. By creating a daily regimen of spiritual

disciplines, along with a physical exercise routine, the believer can systematically build an overcoming walk with the Lord. Whatever we practice, we will ultimately become better at and more confident in our ability to succeed. If we yield to the demands of practice, it will ensure that we will not be lazy or slothful, comfortable, or complacent in our personal development. Some important areas for personal growth we must cultivate are

1. *daily prayer* time with God,
2. *periodic fasting* from food or other social activities,
3. *quiet time* during the day for personal reflection,
4. *journaling*,
5. *studying* the scriptures,
6. reading a daily *devotional booklet*, and
7. the *praise and worship* of the Lord.

These are just a few suggestions, which might help the individual desirous of putting into practice habits that will encourage Christian development and maturity. Always remember, if you want to win in this life, we must be committed to practice our skill until it is refined. Just as an athlete prepares himself to win by mental and physical disciplines, so are we for our Christian race (1 Corinthians 9:24–29).

We need to practice using the gifts of the Holy Spirit (1 Corinthians 12:1–11), as well as the daily habits mentioned above. The more we seek to use the anointing of Christ, the better we will become at administering the Holy Spirit's power and grace.

Reflection Questions

1. Does your philosophy for success in life include the discipline of practice, practice, practice?
2. How often do you practice what you preach to others?
3. What habits or rituals have you discovered are useful for your personal growth and maturity in the Lord?

Spiritual Practices

1. Practice memorizing key passages of scripture that inspire you to have faith in God (ex. Psalms 23 and 91).
2. Practice developing the love of Christ by doing good for someone every Saturday for a month.
3. Commit yourself to practice something in which you have always wanted to become proficient.

Devotional 14

Submission

Obey them that have the rule over you, and submit yourselves: for they watch for your souls, as they that must give account, that they may do it with joy, and not with grief: for that is unprofitable for you.

—Hebrews 13:17

Submission is one of the hardest acts we are asked to do because of man's pride, sin, and need for self-importance. Man's problem with submission is best defined by the word *rebellion*, which is the unwillingness to obey authority. Everyone wants to feel as though they are in control of their destiny or someone else's. Therefore, we struggle to maintain a balance between being submissive and conforming to authority. A true biblical example of this struggle can be seen in Philippians 2:5–10, where Jesus models for us true humility and submission to His Father's authority. See verses 7 and 8, "*But made himself of no reputation, and took upon him the form of a servant and was made in the likeness of men: and being found in fashion as a man, he humbled himself, and became obedient unto death, even the death of the cross.*"

Within these verses is a glimpse of the inner character of Christ and an example of how we are expected to yield to our heavenly Father's authority as we seek to serve him. Jesus, we are told, humbled Himself, not that God humbled Him, but He humbled Himself. We must humble ourselves (Proverbs 6:3, 1 Peter 5:6) as an act of the will by yielding ourselves to the authority of God and men. The ability to submit to authority in the kingdom of God is highly valued because it speaks of trust, faith, self-control, self-discipline, and ultimately points to a person's quality of character. The church today is in desperate need of followers who can mirror Christ's example (John 13:1–17) of service and submission while divorcing ourselves from attitudes of pride and rebellion to authority. Self-importance began in the Garden of Eden (Genesis 3:1–7) and is still at war within the hearts and minds of Christ's followers today. Our position must be that of being able to submit to God, the church leadership, other believers and people in society who are in authority over us (governing officials, police, our boss, etc...).

In every institution, there are abuses of power as this has been well documented throughout human history, but there must be order and submission to authority for the sake of peace. Therefore, we are instructed to pray for those in authority (1 Timothy 2:1–2) and (Matthew 5:44; Luke 6:28) those who mistreat us. Prayer is the key to sustaining a life of submission and humility as we continue to seek and serve the Lord.

Reflection Questions

1. When asked about the word *submission*, what comes to mind?
2. What specific event in your life introduced you to the act of submission?
3. Ask yourself this question, "Do I have a problem submitting to those in authority?"
4. Do I show submission to the Lord in areas of church attendance and tithing?

Spiritual Practices

1. Identify someone in your life who is in authority over you and then evaluate your level of submission to them.

2. Ask yourself every day for a month, "How have I submitted my life to Christ today?"

3. Show your commitment to serving others by submitting your time to help others (at a hospital, homeless shelter, etc. for one day a month).

4. Always remember what Jesus said about authority and submission in Matthew 8:5–13. We are all "under" someone's authority!

Devotional 15

Financial Giving

Give, and it shall be given unto you; good measure, pressed
down, shaken together, and running over, shall men
give into your bosom. For with the same measure that
ye mete withal it shall be measured to you again.

—*Luke 6:38*

One of the most challenging things believers are asked to do, because of the prevalence of greed within society, is to give. The above scripture promises us a tremendous benefit if we simply learn to give in faith to the Lord. God will miraculously cause people to become a resource for our blessing until we are overwhelmed with increase. Many believers struggle to believe this promise along with many others because of selfish desires rooted in greed and lust for material possessions. The Lord has always required that His people learn how to bring Him an offering and why it is necessary (Genesis 4:1–5, 22:2–8, Exodus 18:12, Leviticus 1:2–5, Numbers 5:9, Deuteronomy 12:11–14, Malachi 3:8–12, 1 Corinthians 16:1–3). The command to bring the Lord an offering was instituted by Him in order to reveal our heart attitude, faith, and obedience in service to Him. When our heart toward the Lord and His Church change, it is usually reflected in the areas of personal service and financial giving.

Therefore, our giving serves as a barometer indicating our relationship with Him and the church community.

In fact, we can't bring the Lord what "we feel" we should give Him, but we should be reminded of Cain's example in Genesis 4 and Malachi 3:8–12. Giving the Lord what He requires is essential if we are going to receive His best, grow spiritually and in grace as we continue to walk with Him. If we say, "Trust the Lord," and don't financially support the work of his kingdom, are we then to believe that we are truly submitted and obedient to him? Luke 16:11 says, *"If therefore ye have not been faithful in the unrighteous mammon, who will commit to your trust the true riches?"*

Here, Christ challenges His disciples to do some introspection concerning their honesty, motivations, wisdom, and willingness to part with money (see vs. 13). The primary lesson to be learned from this parable is that we cannot love money and God at the same time because both of them demand our devotion, time, energy, and affection in order to gain a favorable position in life.

Reflection Questions

1. Are you currently tithing (giving 10 percent of your income) to the house of the Lord?
2. Read Matthew 6:19–34. How does this passage shape your understanding of money?

Spiritual Practices

1. Plan to give to a Christian missionary organization this year.
2. Look at your checkbook or bank statement and determine how much you really love God.
3. Volunteer at your local church or some other organization without being financially compensated for your work.

Devotional 16

— ❦ —

Obedience Is the Key!

*And Samuel said, Hath the Lord as great delight in burnt offerings
and sacrifices, as in obeying the voice of the Lord? Behold, to obey
is better than sacrifice, and to hearken than the fat of rams.*

—*1 Samuel 15:22*

In an age in which people are encouraged to do whatever comes
to mind or whatever makes them feel good, the call to obedience
is one that is not being well received. As believers, we are asked to
renounce this type of thinking and living in order to pursue a life of
obedience to Christ. While this calling can be very difficult in today's
society, to the church at Philippi Paul writes of Christ's example,
*"And being found in fashion as a man, humbled himself, and became
obedient unto death, even the death of the cross"* (Philippians 2:8).

This verse is the foundation and strength upon which the
Christian faith is built. Christ as the pattern Son modeled for us how
we are to become obedient unto God, even if it means the death of
our selfish desires. Obedience is what God demands from us if he
is going to use us, promote us, and bless us (Deuteronomy 8:1–3).
He must know that we are totally submitted to his will, anointing,
and power. Becoming obedient is the result of constantly keeping
our flesh (carnal nature) in subjection to Christ and by maintaining
a vibrant prayer and reading life in the Lord. The more scripture we

know and understand (by putting it into practice), the more conviction the Holy Spirit can bring to our lives for the purpose of producing obedient servants for Christ (John 16:8–9, Romans 6:16–17, Galatians 5:17, Hebrews 5:9).

Another powerful benefit for living a life of obedience to the Lord can be found in Deuteronomy 28:1–14 (Leviticus 26:1–13) where the promise of blessing is to be bestowed upon those who wholeheartedly follow Him. Our heavenly Father's deepest desire is to have a relationship with His people based on love, not fear that comes from pending judgment. He longs to see us eager to seek and serve Him, not out of duty. This truth can best be illustrated in the following story adapted from Aretta Loving, "Obedience Is the Better Decision," September 15, 1990.

All Right, Loving

Aretta Loving, Wycliffe missionary, was washing her breakfast dishes when she saw Jimmy, the five-year-old neighbor, headed straight toward the back porch. She had just finished painting the back porch handrails, and she was proud of her work.

"Come around to the front door, Jimmy," she shouted. "There's wet paint on the porch rails."

"I'll be careful," Jimmy replied, not turning from his path.

"No, Jimmy! Don't come up the steps," Aretta shouted, knowing of Jimmy's tendency to mess things up.

"I'll be careful," he said again, by now dangerously close to the steps.

"Jimmy stop!" Aretta shouted. "I don't want carefulness. I want obedience!"

As the words burst from her mouth, she suddenly remembered Samuel's response to King Saul, "To obey is better than sacrifice."

How would Jimmy respond? Aretta wondered.

To her relief, he shouted back, "All right, Loving, I'll go around to the front door."

He was the only one who called her by her last name like that, and it had endeared him to her from the beginning.

As he turned around the house, Aretta thought to herself, "How often am I like Saul or like Jimmy, wanting to go my own way? I rationalize, 'I'll be careful, Lord,' as I proceed with my own plans."

But He doesn't want carefulness. He wants obedience. How often do we find ourselves feeling like Aretta? The key to being obedient is to realize 1 Samuel 15:22's truth. That it is far better to obey the Lord the first time than to disobey and have to offer Him a sacrifice (which is a way of saying, "I'm sorry.").

Remember, "When God puts a period, do not change it to a question mark."

Obedience is the key!

Reflection Questions

1. Do you believe yourself to be a person who is obedient?
2. Does your lifestyle reflect your obedience to the Word of God?
3. What is the last thing you feel the Lord has asked you to do, and have you done it?

Spiritual Practices

1. Take a moment to evaluate your attitude when someone in authority asks you to do something you feel or don't feel like doing.
2. Meet with someone you trust and discuss some of the challenges you have with being disobedient to the Lord or people in authority.
3. Read and reflect on the following scriptures:
   a) 1 Samuel 15:22
   b) Psalm 139:23
   c) Hebrews 13:17
   d) Colossians 3:18–24
   e) 1 Peter 5:6

Devotional 17

Church Attendance

And let us consider one another to provoke unto love and to good works: not forsaking the assembling of ourselves together, as the manner of some is, but exhorting one another: and so much the more, as you see the day approaching.

—Hebrews 10:24–25

The call of God for His people to gather together has been an ongoing occurrence from the beginning of human history. It began with Adam and Eve in the Garden (Genesis 3:8–9); it was the excuse Moses used to tell Pharaoh to "let my people go" (Exodus 3:18), and it was evident in Numbers 10:1–10 where God called His people together when they heard the sound of the trumpet. It was the *call to assemble* in a specific place in order to commune with Him. Over the centuries, the calling to assemble hasn't changed but, in fact, has been encouraged because of our need to commune with the Lord, as well as strengthen one another in the faith. Many today don't hold this view due to an independent-isolation perspective society is modeling before us. Believers start to practice not coming together more and more; therefore, leaving themselves vulnerable to spiritual attacks, depression, feelings of hopelessness, and a lost sense of love, which comes from a lack of interaction with people who are like-minded in Christ. Hebrews 10:25 emphasizes the importance of not becoming isolated as we see the day of the Lord's coming due to a heightened increase of sin all around us (Matthew 24:1–51, 2 Timothy 3: 1–9).

Our weekly need for assembling with fellow believers should never be understated. Every time the doors of the church are opened, we must see the need to be assembled together. This includes:

1.   Encouraging each other (Hebrew 10:25)
2.   Loving one another (Galatians 5:13–14)
3.   Sharing the burdens of others (Galatians 6:1–2)

When people say that they can "have church by themselves at home," they are not embracing the understanding or power inherent in fellowshipping within the Body of Christ, nor do they understand the sacrament of Holy Communion (1 Corithians 11). We are not at the table of the Lord (Matthew 26:26–29) alone, but with the Lord and other believers as we celebrate the body and blood of Christ, which is the key to our redemption. Assembling ourselves together is not an option as some would like to think, but it is the highest priority set forth by the law, Christ, and the Apostle Paul as evidenced in both the testaments. Psalm 133 testifies to the benefit of God's family coming together because it fosters unity, peace, and the anointing of the Holy Spirit. This truth can be found embedded in Isaiah 65:8, which says, "*Thus saith the Lord, 'As the new wine is found in the cluster, and one saith, Destroy it not; for a blessing is in it: so will I do for my servants' sakes, that I may not destroy them all.'*"

Herein is the mystery revealed to all who ask, "Why is it important to assemble together?" The "new wine" (the Holy Spirit, Acts 2:1–4, 13) and the "cluster" (assembling in fellowship together) is where strength, healing, peace, and the anointing can be found!

Reflection Questions

1.   How serious is your devotion to attending weekly church services?

2. While at church, what activities are you involved in?
3. What hinders you when you don't attend services, and is it in your opinion a valid excuse?
4. If you were to search your heart, can you say that you attend service to be taught, worship, and fellowship, or are there other reasons?

Spiritual Practices

1. Despite weather conditions, commit to attending every service over the next two months.
2. Attend prayer and Bible study meetings for one month.
3. Try contacting someone that you have not seen at church for a while and motivate them to return as soon as possible.
4. Financially support your church through tithing (10 percent of your income).
5. Join a volunteer ministry of your church and be a source of encouragement to the organization/group.

Devotional 18

ᴄᴘ

Faithfulness

*He that is faithful in that which is least is faithful also in much:
and he that is unjust in the least is unjust also in much.*

—*Luke 16:10*

According to *Webster's Dictionary*, faithfulness is defined as "the quality of being faithful, loyalty, constancy in affection, fidelity." Therefore, to be faithful a person is said to be (1) "full of faith, believing, strong or firm in one's faith, especially religious faith," and (2) firmly adhering to duty of true fidelity, loyal, true to allegiance, constant in performance of duties or services, honest, loyal, as a faithful servant." Throughout the Bible, much is said about the quality of faithfulness because it is a virtue that many people don't possess and should be trying to obtain. This quality is of high priority to God because He needs committed people to fulfill His plans and who have a right perspective on being His servant throughout the process. Faithfulness in essence is a leadership virtue, which ultimately separates "doers from hearers" (Matthew 21:28–31) time and time again. Churches need people that can be counted on to fulfill their duty without excuses, drama, or complaint, and who don't necessarily need an award to be given them at the completion of their job.

Jesus often addressed the topic of faithfulness when He sought to instill a new set of values for His disciples as He hoped to transform their minds and character (Matthew 24:44–51, Matthew 25:21, Luke 12:35–48, Luke 19:17). Jesus knew that for Him to be able to impact the world with His kingdom message, He was going to need the help of dedicated, faithful followers He could depend on, even when facing a crisis. Faithfulness is the key to any great person or plan one may have envisioned because when all is said and done, it is what will keep you focused and enthusiastic about completing the task at hand.

> *Old Faithful is not the largest geyser in Yellowstone National Park, nor does it reach the greatest height. But it is by far the most popular one. Why? It is regular and dependable, hence its name, "Old Faithful." (Anonymous)*

The individual who has proven to be faithful over the least things (job, money, possessions, etc…) will most often be trustworthy over the much (positions of authority, abundant possessions, wealth and prosperity, etc…). When we pray and ask the Lord for more, we need to evaluate what we have been doing with least and then try to understand why this prayer is not being answered. Faithfulness is a kingdom principle, which the Lord uses when determining our advancement growth and maturity in Him. For this reason, we ask ourselves these questions:

Reflection Questions

1. How faithful have I been with what the Lord has entrusted to me?
2. Do others consider me to be full of faith (hence faithful), or am I a person who only sees the bad in most things?
3. When you have obligated yourself to do something and then you have a change of heart, are you faithful to your initial commitment?
4. Can others count on you to be there on time and ready to work with a right attitude?

Spiritual Practices

1. Sign up for an upcoming church event and be faithful to attend the function.
2. Take a moment to review all of the checks you have written over the past three months and see how much has been given to the work of God.
3. Make a list of the things the Lord has done for you over the past year in order to reflect upon his faithfulness.
4. Please read and reflect on Luke 16:10–12.

Devotional 19

—— ✑ ——

Endurance

Thou therefore endure hardness, as a good soldier of Jesus Christ.

—*2 Timothy 2:3*

Endurance can be defined as (1) continuing existence, persistence, and (2) uninterrupted or lasting existence, continuation. While the word *endure* means (1) to come to a knowledge of (something) by living through it, experience, and (2) to put up with (something painful or difficult. Both of these definitions convey a sense of being able to continually bear difficulties experienced without giving up. The Apostle Paul illustrates for us how to endure difficulties in life and in ministry in 2 Corinthians 11:21–33, where he explains the sufferings he faced while preaching the gospel of the kingdom. His many challenges are recorded to help prove his commitment, calling, and purpose in his service to the Lord as an apostle. Paul's advice to Timothy is to be strong in his ministry calling and to endure difficulties as a soldier, which is responsible to handle hardness in his walk with the Lord. Problems, challenges, hardships, and the like are always hindrances God's servants' face, but we learn how to endure life's circumstances and it can benefit us by:

1. Changing our perspective on life.
2. Building an inner determination to finish what we have started.

3. Teaching us to have faith and trust only in the Lord.
4. Helping us to understand God's grace.
5. Building character virtues (Galatians 5:22–23).
6. Showing us our need to deepen our relationship with Christ who is our strength (John 15:5).
7. Preparing us to do the will of God (Philippians 2:13).
8. Revealing our level of personal growth in Him (2 Peter 1:2–11).

Ultimately, we should become stronger. These are just a few benefits you can clearly see can come from the blessed quality of endurance. Let's read this story:

> *I was talking with a farmer about his soybean and corn crops. Rain had been abundant, and the results were evident. So his comment surprised me.*
>
> *"My crops are especially vulnerable. Even a short drought could have a devastating effect."*
>
> *"Why?" I asked.*
>
> *He explained that while we see the frequent rains as a benefit, during that time, the plants are not required to push roots deeper in search of water. The roots remain near the surface. A drought would find the plants unprepared and quickly kill them.*
>
> *Some Christians receive abundant "rains" of worship, fellowship, and teaching. Yet when stress enters their lives, many suddenly abandon God or think Him unfaithful. Their roots have never pushed much below the surface. Only roots grown deep into God (Colossians 2:6–7) help us endure times of drought in our lives. (Neil Orchard)*

It is noteworthy to see the correlation between life's problems and our willingness to endure these seasons of testing. Many believers are tempted to give up and turn back when faced with severe obstacles on their journey with the Lord, but we are not of them who "turn back" (Luke 9:62, Hebrews 10:38). Individuals who are determined to have a fruitful life in the Spirit must anticipate spiritual warfare and equip themselves accordingly as discussed in Ephesians 6:10–18, which is a scripture dealing with the "soldier-saint" who is prepared for battle. Never allow excessive times of seasonal drought to overwhelm you but seek the Lord, draw nigh to Him, and keep your faith in the Lord Jesus Christ who will see you through.

Reflection Questions

1. What have you endured over the past nine months?
2. Ask this question of yourself, "Am I a finisher of what I start?"
3. Is patience an evident quality in your life while enduring a difficult situation? (Be specific)

Spiritual Practices

1. Study the life of Job and note every challenge presented to him throughout his nine-month ordeal and see how he endured difficult circumstances.
2. During the trials of life, read a Psalm in the morning and read a Proverb at night in order to give you wisdom and peace.
3. Intentionally focus your prayer time with the Lord and ask for His wisdom and strength.
4. Determine within yourself that your situation is not going to get the best of you because your faith is in the Lord alone.

Devotional 20

Let the River Flow

In the last day, that great day of the feast, Jesus stood and cried, saying, If any man thirst, let him come unto me, and drink. He that believeth on me, as the scripture hath said, out of his belly shall flow rivers of living water. (But this spake he of the Spirit, which they that believe on him should receive: for the Holy Ghost was not yet given; because that Jesus was not yet glorified.

—John 7:37–39

Jesus gave a wonderful promise to His disciples that would continue to believe in Him. He said that out of our belly (innermost being, our hearts) would flow rivers of living water (the supernatural reserve of the Holy Spirit). It literally meant that every believer would be able to tap into the resources of God's Spirit to bring life and healing to anyone in need, and this promise found its initial fulfillment in Acts 2:1–4, 38, which was the feast day of Pentecost. Christ's vision for His Church was to reproduce His anointing and ability in the lives of every one of His followers and to have them to be streams of life to a thirsty, dying world (Isaiah 55:1, Matthew 5:6, John 4:13–14, 6:25, 7:37, Revelation 7:16). Also, in Ezekiel 47:1–10, there is a prophetic statement by the prophet, which confirms Christ's promise. A river of life was to flow from the temple doors into a desolate world bringing hope, healing, and restoration.

The Apostle Paul understood prophetic imagery and cited a scripture, which says to the followers of Christ, "Know ye not that your body is the temple of the Holy Ghost" (1 Corinthians 6:15–20, see I Corinthians 3:17), which is, in fact, the revelation of Ezekiel's temple in scripture. It is important to see the effects of the river on people or objects, which come in contact with it (Ezekiel 47:8–9). This river flows from a temple, who we are (1 Corinthians 3:16) and is expected to be available to flow from believers in the home, on a job, or any place where needs abound.

Remember, wherever you go, whatever you do, "Let the river flow."

Reflection Questions

1. What do you do to maintain the flow of the river of life from you to those in need?
2. Honestly, are you filled with the Holy Spirit's love and grace until you are overflowing?
3. When is the last time you allowed the river of life to impact a lost soul?

Spiritual Practices

1. Spend thirty minutes a day for ten days worshipping and praising the Lord.
2. Volunteer some of your time to a social organization.
3. Meet in a group of three to five people and discuss ways you use to allow the "river to flow" in your life.
4. Seek the Lord for the baptism of the Holy Spirit and for more of His power in your life.

Devotional 21

Desiring Spirituality

Follow after charity, and desire spiritual gifts,
but rather that ye may prophecy.

—*1 Corinthians 14:1*

The above scripture reading should serve as motivation for any believer who aspires to use the gifts of the Holy Spirit. The Apostle Paul tells us to "desire: these gifts along with the balance of charity (love). The Hebrew word for "desire" is (*zēloō*), which according to Strong's Concordance means "to have warmth of feelings for or against, affect, covet (earnestly), (have) desire, (move with) envy, be jealous over, (be) zealous (by affect)." In essence, it means to earnestly crave for something much like the running deer desires to drink water (Psalm 42:1–2). Soulful desire for something is always a driving force, which propels an individual forward until they accomplish their goal, and so it is with being used by the Holy Spirit. A casual attitude involving the work of the Holy Spirit usually yields little or no fruit, but the person who continues to seek after the Lord and His kingdom will be rewarded (Isaiah 55:6, Jeremiah 29:13, Matthew 7:7, Luke 11:9).

When seeking the gifts of the Holy Spirit for a greater anointing for ministry, believers must diligently "crave" the experience while always maintaining a heart of faith, obedience, and love in order to be found faithful for Christ's empowerment. There will be many obstacles designed by Satan to hinder our growth and usage in the kingdom of God, but we must remain focused on the prize at hand and persevere until we have apprehended His grace. Catering to diligent times of prayer, fasting, worship, the study of the scriptures, and walking in love are key components for anyone desirous of moving in the power of God.

Remember to *"crave"* spiritual giftings! (Please read 1 Corinthians 12:1–11).

Reflection Questions

1. Do you deeply desire spirituality or is it something you can live without?
2. What do you do to sharpen your spiritual gifts on a regular basis?
3. Ask a friend to evaluate your level of spirituality on a scale of 1 to 10, and then ask them how they arrived at that number?

Spiritual Practices

1. Choose four biblical characters and rate their level of spirituality on a scale of 1 to 10.
2. Fast from food for a period of twelve to twenty-four hours one day a week.
3. Chart your spiritual journey over the last two years and see how much you have grown.
4. Create a two-day spiritual retreat where you can commune with the Lord in deep reflection and journal about the experience.

Devotional 22

—— ⚜ ——

Growing In Grace

But grow in grace, and in the knowledge of our Lord and Saviour
Jesus Christ. To him be glory both now and forever. Amen.

—2 Peter 3:18

The Apostle Paul exhorts believers to "grow in grace," which is a cry for the church to accept the unmerited kindness of God given to benefit believers in their service to him. The Greek meaning of "grace" is "joy, favor, acceptance, a kindness granted or desired, a benefit, thanks, gratitude. A favor done without expectation of return, absolute freeness of the loving-kindness of God to men, finding its only motive in the bounty and free heartedness of the Giver, unearned and unmerited favor." It is this unexpected gratitude that becomes strength to those in need of help and manifests itself by the empowerment of God's Spirit. In 2 Corinthians, we can see an example of this when Paul prayed three times to have this "thorn in the flesh" removed.

The Lord responded to him by saying, *"For this thing I besought the Lord thrice, that it might depart from me. And he said unto me, My grace is sufficient for thee: for my strength is made perfect in weakness. Most gladly therefore will I rather glory in my infirmities, that the power of Christ may rest upon me. Therefore, I take pleasure in infirmities, in reproaches, in necessities, in persecutions, in distresses for Christ's sake: for when I am weak, then am I strong"* (2 Corinthians 9:8–10).

Someone once said, "Mercy doesn't give me what I do deserve, while grace gives me what I don't deserve." What a profound statement this is. Like Paul, we all need to know that the Lord's ever-present help and strength is always available to us no matter how far we have fallen away from him. It is his love and grace that must continue to grow in us through the discipline of studying to obtain the "knowledge that will sustain us during difficult times and will reassure us of God's provision of grace."

In his book, *In the Grip of Grace*, Max Lucado writes:

> *In my first church, we had more than our share of southern ladies who loved to cook. I fit in well because I was a single guy who loved to eat. Our potlucks were major events.*
>
> *I counted on those potluck dinners for my survival. While others were planning what to cook, I was studying my kitchen shelves to see what I could offer. The result was pitiful. One of my better offerings was an unopened sack of chips. Another time, I took a half-empty jar of peanuts.*
>
> *Wasn't much, but no one ever complained. Those ladies would take my jar of peanuts and set it on the long table with the rest of the food and hand me a plate. "Go ahead. Don't be bashful. Fill up your plate." And I would! Mashed potatoes and gravy. Roast beef. Fried chicken.*
>
> *I came like a pauper and ate like a king!*
>
> *The Apostle Paul would have loved the symbolism of those potlucks. He would say that Christ does for us precisely what those women did for me.*

This story helps to illustrate how grace simply is made available to meet our needs and to remind us of God's *amazing grace*.

Reflection Questions

1. In which areas of your life do you need to experience more of the grace of God?
2. How is the grace of God connected to the knowledge of God (see 2 Peter 3:18)?
3. Have you helped someone lately to utilize the available grace of God?

Spiritual Practices

1. Make a list of events when you experienced the grace of God.
2. Find someone in need and minister out of your knowledge and experiences of God's grace.
3. For the next seven days, pray for more of God's grace in your life.

Devotional 23

Serving Others

And there was also a strife among them, which of them should be accounted the greatest. And he said unto them, The kings of the Gentiles exercise authority upon them are called benefactors. But ye shall not be so: but he that is greatest among you. Let him be as the younger; and he that is chief, as he that doth serve. For whatever is greater, he that sitteth at meat, or he that serveth? Is not he that sitteth at meat? But I am among you as he that serveth.

—Luke 22:24–27

The idea of serving others is not necessarily a dominant Western mindset, which prevails in our culture. We have been taught that to be in charge (a leader) is the normal acceptable standard to live life, and to be a servant of others is demeaning and counterproductive to the idea of success. Most people do not aspire to be the servants of society, but instead are driven to become leaders within every phase of society. When people are born into God's kingdom, their value and belief systems are immediately challenged by the teachings of Christ, who calls every disciple He uses to become a servant of all. In Luke 22:24–27, Jesus confronts the mindset of dominant leadership by contrasting the two. He ultimately explains that His follower should never seek to dominate others for the sake of exercising authority over them. Instead, He encouraged them to serve others because this is the true essence of greatness.

In John 13:4–16 is the story of how Jesus washed the disciples' feet as He took on the outward role of a servant in order to convey an inward reality of what was in His heart that of a servant. His example is to act as a blueprint for believers to follow as they seek to become like their Lord. Unless we come to an understanding of what benefit serving others yields for our lives, we will never come to the reality of Christ's work on earth. Some of these benefits include the development of compassion, humility of heart, the ability to be long-suffering, and patient in all things. Another main benefit of serving is that it reveals the "dark secrets" of the heart and ugly attitudes toward others who will usually remain hidden from plain sight. A serving spirit is what we need to ask the Lord for if we intend on changing the world for Christ.

God did not save you to be a sensation. He saved you to be a servant. (Anonymous)

Let us follow our Lord's example by being a servant of humanity.

Bruce Thielemann, pastor of First Presbyterian Church in Pittsburgh, told of a conversation with an active layman, who mentioned, *"You preachers talk a lot about giving, but when you get right down to it, it all comes down to basin theology."*

Thielemann asked, *"Basin theology? What's that?"*

The layman replied, *"Remember what Pilate did when he had the chance to acquit Jesus? He called for a basin and washed his hands of the whole thing. But Jesus, the night before His death, called for a basin and proceeded to wash the feet of the disciples. It all comes down to basin theology. Which one will you use?"*

Reflection Questions

1. How have you served others over the past three months?
2. What volunteer ministries of your church do you participate in?

3. Is it obvious to others that you are indeed a servant in mind, body, and spirit?
4. Are you willing to serve in the most menial positions available, or do you aspire to the most visible and rewarding positions at home, work, and church?

Spiritual Practices

1. Serve your family by volunteering to wash dishes for a month or by doing some other chore around the house.
2. Propose that your church have a foot-washing service (John 13).
3. One Saturday a month, do some good deed for a neighbor.

Devotional 24

— ❧ —

Be Holy!

*As obedient children, not fashioning yourselves according
to the former lusts in your ignorance: but as he who hath
called you is holy, so be ye holy in all manner of conversation;
because it is written, be ye holy; for I am holy.*

—*1 Peter 1:14–16*

One of the most neglected aspects of Christian living today is
that of holiness. We are commanded throughout scripture to
live a life that is holy because it is one of the greatest attributes of
God that He expects to be exhibited in those who follow Him. Peter
uses an Old Testament usage of the word holy and presents it to
New Testament believers of His day. The word used is "*hagios*" (holy)
which means "*holy, set apart, sanctified, consecrated. It has a common
root, hag, with hagnós (53), chaste, pure. Its fundamental ideas are separation, consecration, devotion to God and sharing in God's purity and
abstaining from earth's defilement*" (Luke 9:26, 2 Peter 1:8).

The main idea Peter is exhorting believers to do is to keep themselves clean and separate from the ungodliness, filth, and defilements
of this world's systems. Believers have been partakers of God's divine
nature (2 Peter 1:4), which in essence is purity and holiness of heart,
mind, and personal conduct. It is this nature that is being developed
in us, and it is one of the main reasons why we have been given the

Holy Spirit. It is his job to transform us into Christ's image (John 16:7–11, Ephesians 4:24, Romans 8:29, 2 Corinthians 3:18). By studying the word of God, along with the power of the Holy Spirit, the possibility of being free to live an overcoming life in Christ is achievable. The Apostle Paul also believed in living a holy and separate life in Christ when he wrote:

> *And what agreement hath the temple of God with idols? For ye are the temple of the living God; as God hath said, I will dwell in them; and I will be their God, and they shall be my people. Wherefore come out from among them, and be ye separate, saith the Lord, and touch not the unclean thing; and I will receive you. (2 Corinthians 6:16–17)*

> *For God hath not called us unto uncleanness, but unto holiness. (1 Thessalonians 4:7)*

The writer of the book of Hebrews also warns us of the importance of living a holy life by saying, "*Follow peace with all men, and holiness, without which no man shall see the Lord*" (Hebrews 12:14).

All of these scriptures should send a message to the believer that our God is holy, and He expects us to be holy if we want to have a fruitful and blessed life now and in the life to come.

> *Many trees appear to be healthy when we see them in summer. But, in the winter, after their leaves have all fallen off, we sometimes find that hidden underneath the lush green of the summer foliage was a parasitic plant called mistletoe, which had been slowly sucking away some of the tree's vitality. We as Christians sometimes have hidden sins, which, like the mistletoe, slowly suck away our spiritual vitality. Although not always evident in times of outward spiritual health and fruitfulness, we must always examine ourselves for those small, often unseen, par-*

asites of sinful habits that will sap our vitality. And we must also remember that just because they are not apparent now does not mean that in another season of our lives God will not reveal them for all to see. (Author unknown)

Reflection Questions

1. What is your understanding of holiness, and how does it govern your decisions in life?
2. As a believer, what are your views on smoking, drunkenness, adultery, abortion, or premarital sex?
3. Do you consider yourself to be holy? Why? How?
4. Are the people you spend the most of your time around considered to be holy? (Because they influence you more than you think.)

Spiritual Practices

1. Make a list of your vices based on your knowledge of the Holy Scriptures, then note the top three in order.
2. Use one day a week to reflect on the topic of holiness and search the Bible for suitable passages to strengthen you in a particular area of weakness.
3. Spend time in prayer and confess your shortcomings to the Lord as you petition Him for His mercy and grace.
4. Practice the spiritual discipline of "silence" as you seek to turn off all media sources so that you can focus more on the Lord.

Notes

Notes

Notes

About the Author

———— ⟡ ————

Rev. Dr. Keith Attles is the founding Pastor of Covenant Life Ministries Church located in Teaneck, NJ. Covenant Life Ministries is a multi-cultural diverse congregation of people from various backgrounds that form a loving fellowship and covenant community. Dr. Attles and his wife Pastor Kimberly, have three children, Aaron, Daniel, and Alisa.

Dr. Attles has ministered in churches and the mission field along the Eastern seaboard, from Boston to the Bahamas, West Indies as well as Jarabacoa, Domincian Republic, Guyana, South America and Fiji, South Pacific. He has a tremendous teaching gift as well as a powerful prophetic and healing ministry.

Dr. Attles received his Doctor of Ministry degree in Leadership and Spiritual Formation from Regent University in Virginia Beach, VA; a Masters in Theology from Alliance Theological Seminary in Nyack, NY and holds a Bachelors of Science Degree in Marketing from Fairleigh Dickinson University, Teaneck, NJ.

Ministry Highlights

- Covenant Life Ministries Church founded in 1995
- Church Planter, Presbyter, and Consultant
- Founder of Ministry Training Academy (MTA) which equips leaders and lay-leaders for ministry service and outreach.

- Adjunct Professor-Alliance Theological Seminary Nyack College, Nyack, NY
- Workshop Presenter and Revivalist
- Korean Seminary Instructor 2001–2004
- Foreign Missions Leadership and Church Development Speaker

CPSIA information can be obtained
at www.ICGtesting.com
Printed in the USA
LVHW032359260422
717239LV00007B/367

9 781639 031535